So Far from the Bamboo Grove

and Related Readings

McDougal Littell
A HOUGHTON MIFFLIN COMPANY
Evanston, Illinois   *Boston*   *Dallas*

Acknowledgments

William Morrow & Company, Inc.: *So Far from The Bamboo Grove* by Yoko Kawashima Watkins. Copyright © 1986 by Yoko Kawashima Watkins. Reprinted by permission of Lothrop, Lee & Shepard Books, a division of William Morrow & Company, Inc.

Doubleday and Harold Ober Associates, Inc.: "Refugee Mother and Child," from *Christmas in Biafra and Other Poems* by Chinua Achebe. Copyright © 1973 by Chinua Achebe. Used by permission of Doubleday, a division of Bantam Doubleday Dell Publishing Group, Inc., and by permission of Harold Ober Associates, Inc.

Simon & Schuster, Inc.: "Old Man at the Bridge," from *The Short Stories of Ernest Hemingway* by Ernest Hemingway. Copyright 1938 by Ernest Hemingway. Copyright renewed © 1966 by Mary Hemingway. Reprinted with the permission of Scribner, a division of Simon & Schuster, Inc.

HarperCollins Publishers: Chapter 11 from *The Endless Steppe* by Esther Hautzig. Copyright © 1968 by Esther Hautzig. Reprinted by permission of HarperCollins Publishers.

Maia Wojciechowska: "The First Day of the War," from *Till the Break of Day* by Maia Wojciechowska. Reprinted by permission of the author.

Rowan Tree Press: "The Key" by Võ Phiên, from *Landscape and Exile*, edited by Marguerite Bouvard. Reprinted by permission of Rowan Tree Press, Boston, Mass.

Addison Wesley Longman: "Please Don't Leave" by Mr. Lue Lee, from *Tales of Courage, Tales of Dreams: A Multicultural Reader* by John Mundahl. Copyright © 1993 by Addison Wesley Publishing Company. Reprinted by permission of Addison Wesley Longman.

Cover illustration by Chi Chung.

ISBN 0-395-77138-2

34567—QNT—   00 99 98 97

Contents

So Far from the Bamboo Grove

Yoko Kawashima Watkins

Chapter 1

It was almost midnight on July 29, 1945, when my mother, my elder sister Ko, and I, carrying as many of our belongings as we could on our backs, fled our home in its bamboo grove, our friends, and our town, Nanam, in northern Korea, forever.

In darkness Mother checked windows and doors. I was eleven, Ko sixteen. I was very tired and my head was so dizzy I did not know which way I was heading. The cool night air swept my face; still my head was not clear. I saw Mother close the main entrance and lock it.

"Now give me your wrist, Little One," she commanded in a low voice.

I was called "Little One" by my parents and Ko, but my older brother, Hideyo, always teasing, called me "Noisy One" because I often screamed when I was teased and when we frolicked in the house.

My wrist? I hadn't had a night's sleep in two weeks because of the air raids. My head was very hazy.

"Hurry!" Mother found my wrist in the darkness. She was tying a rope to it. "So I won't lose you."

Tying Ko's wrist, she asked, her voice full of worry, "You did leave a note for your father?"

"Yes, Mother."

"I left a note for Hideyo," said Mother. "Oh, I hope he finds it and joins us. He can get in through his window. Now remember, no one knows we are leaving. No matter what, until we reach the train station, be silent. Understand?"

"Yes," Ko said again. I wanted to cry.

Though we lived in northeastern Korea, we were

Japanese. My country, Japan, which I had never seen, had been fighting America and Britain for four years. Because Father was a Japanese government official, working in Manchuria, I had grown up in this ancient town. We were fifty miles from the Manchurian border, and we were so close to the Russian ports, Vladivostok and Nakhodka, across the sea from our harbor. Father came home by train as often as he could.

The shadow of war had been creeping across our peaceful village for months. The most horrible shock had come some weeks before. Mother and I were alone and I was practicing my brush-writing before going to my teacher's house for a calligraphy lesson. Calligraphy is dipping a fat or thin brush in India ink and writing in script or in the square style of Chinese characters.

I had finished my final copy when four Japanese army police burst in through the main door of our house, which only invited guests used, without taking off their shoes.

A mean-looking policeman told Mother, "We are here to collect metal. Iron, bronze, silver, and gold."

Mother stood, bewildered, and he yelled at her.

She gave him Father's treasured silver ashtray set. He threw it in a box and demanded, "More!"

Mother brought her bronze flower vase that stood in the *Tokonoma* (alcove), where flowers were always elegantly arranged. She began to pull the lovely arrangement of irises out one by one, and the policeman pushed her, yanked out the irises and leaves, and dumped the vase and heavy metal frog inside into the box. Mother's eyes were fixed on that box, but she was silent.

The head one noticed Mother's wedding ring and he demanded that. Then her spectacles, gold-rimmed, though she told him she could see nothing without them. They went into the box.

Finally the head police picked up the Mount Fuji paperweight holding my calligraphy copy. That paperweight had been sent to me by Father's mother. She said it had been passed on to my father from way back and she could still see my father, when young, using it to practice brush-writing. Through this Mount Fuji paperweight I dreamed of seeing the majestic mountain and imagined the beauty of my homeland.

He glanced at my writing, *"Bu Un Cho Kyu"* (Good Luck in War), then left the sheet and tossed the paperweight into the box.

I had stood there helpless, fists clenched, seething, and the iron weight smashing Mother's important lenses released my fury. I jumped at the head policeman's hand and bit it as hard as I could.

He yelled, but I bit harder. He shook me off, pushed Mother away and made her fall. Then he threw me on the floor and kicked my side and back with heavy army boots that had hard soles with metal cleats. My head went dark. Somewhere in the dark space I heard Mother's anguished cry. "Leave . . . leave!"

When I awoke, Hideyo, Ko, Mother, and Doctor Yamada were around me. The doctor was a friend of Father's who always treated his patients with a smile, but not this time. He gave me a shot.

Mother was putting a cold towel on my back. Every time I took a deep breath my chest and side pained, and the doctor said I might have cracked ribs. He looked at me through his half-glasses. "No more frolicking, no more crossing the stream. You stay home until I say all right."

He turned to Mother. "I will call my optometrist

friend and he will prescribe lenses for you. This is absolutely inexcusable of the military," he said angrily. "The government must be desperate for supplies to make ammunition. Telephone me if a thing like this happens again."

His bald head was shining against the late afternoon sun, and in spite of my misery I remembered what he had said to Father once when he came to the New Year's party—that he must invent a solution to grow black wavy hair.

I was glad I did not have to go to school the next day. For a long time, school had been changing. We studied for only three periods, and the male teachers were wearing army uniforms. Women and girls had to wear the national clothes, by order of Japanese Prime Minister Tojo—khaki pants gathered at the ankles, simply designed long-sleeved blouses.

For part of our school day we would do labor service for the army, collecting empty cans or going to the ammunition squadron to sort flawed bullets from large boxes, wearing stiff army gloves. I hated that work. Mother often said she did not like killing, and I felt I was helping the army kill people, even though they were our enemies.

Whenever Father came home, he and Hideyo worked, digging a shelter in the thicket large enough for the whole family to crawl into.

"Why, Father?" I asked.

"Just in case of an air raid. It's wartime." He sent Ko and me to find tall thin bamboo shoots and tie strings around bundles of them, to make a cover for the shelter.

He also told us to pack emergency rucksacks, with rice, dried fish, a mess kit, some changes of clothing, and a blanket each. He said these should be left at the main entrance so that if a raid came we could each grab our own and run to the shelter.

For herself Mother prepared a huge double wrapping cloth. Besides emergency items she put in important papers such as our health records, insurance policies, and even report cards from school.

I saw her sewing on her cloth. "What are you doing, Mother?"

"I am making pockets."

"What for?"

"For various things."

The pupils began digging ditches around the school in case an air raid came and we had no time to get home. I was given a shovel, but the handle was much taller than I and heavy. I could not dig that hard rocky ground. I huffed and puffed, just wrestling with the shovel.

We learned which siren was an alert and which an all-clear. We were digging when our first air raid alarm came. The alert siren burst out; our teacher, Mr. Enomoto, shouted, ordering everyone to flatten on the ground. I heard engines roaring over my head.

I had never seen an airplane, but when I looked up, I saw clearly: American planes in formations of three flying over us. Mr. Enomoto yelled at me to put my head down. His scream was angry and frightening. My heart raced, and, face down, I breathed heavily, my breath scattering the dirt around my mouth. When the all-clear sounded I wanted to go home, but we continued to dig.

When I did get home I was exhausted, and I could not concentrate on my calligraphy lesson. My hands were still shaking from handling the shovel, and I could not hold the brush steady. My first air raid experience, and Father was not home! I felt very insecure.

Even with the war upon us, my parents insisted

that I continue with all my special lessons, not only calligraphy but The Way of Tea—an art of serving and receiving tea—flower arrangement, poetry writing and reading, and Japanese classic dance lessons. After that first air raid I asked Mother if I might be excused from all the extra lessons from now on and just be at home with her.

"You mean to quit?" she asked.

"I am not talented in any of my lessons. Besides, I am so tired."

"Your being talented or not doesn't matter," said Mother. "This learning will be useful someday. And the lessons help polish your mind. As for being tired, just go to bed early."

I thought back to the terrible news that had come from our homeland in April. The last school bell of the day had rung on a warm sleepy afternoon. We all stood and bowed to Mr. Enomoto and he returned the bow. He reminded us of our cleaning assignments. Then, pale and serious, he broke the news.

"I am sorry to tell you, but American bombers have attacked Tokyo and the city is demolished. How many of you have relatives in that city?"

A few classmates raised their hands. "I am sorry," Mr. Enomoto said, looking at each one in turn. "The noon news was that almost all of the people are dead. Tokyo is a billow of fire."

Children began sobbing. I felt terrible for them, but I was relieved that my grandparents lived in northern Japan.

I wanted to get home fast to be with Mother. How I wished we did not have those cleaning assignments, but my group, ten of us, had to clean the first graders' classroom and their toilets, as usual.

As soon as the cleaning was over I dashed outdoors.

I took a shortcut home. As I ran down the grassy bank, sparrows rose suddenly and flew away into the high deep blue sky, humming as they went. The tributary of the Tumen River ran swiftly, bouncing around large rocks and leaving sparkling beads.

I took off my shoes and stockings and stuffed them in my pockets. I walked in the shallow stream of the river, then straight into the bamboo grove, and ran all the way home.

"Mother! Tokyo is demolished!" I cried.

My family, unlike most in Nanam, had a radio. "I know." Mother's shoulders drooped. "I only hope the fighting will not spread to us." She sighed deeply. "I've just heard that the army has established another division at the foot of Kyojo Hill." That was only a mile from us. "Also, the Imperial Navy is docking warships in Rashin." Thirty miles away. "And," she went on reporting, "the army has taken farming land from the Koreans by force to expand the army hospital. Little One, the Koreans have established a group they call the Anti-Japanese Communist Army." The Koreans were part of the Japanese empire but they hated the Japanese and were not happy about the war.

"It's terrifying," Mother said.

Then she changed the subject, away from war. "Your performing day at the hospital is tomorrow. Why don't you practice before supper?"

I was one of the children who had been chosen to perform for the wounded soldiers at the army hospital. Dancing lessons were something Father had decided Ko and I should take, and I detested them. I had to give up play time. My unwillingness showed in the many mistakes I made in steps or in lifting my leg when I should not, or skipping a turn. The teacher, Mr. Fukui, sang the difficult notes of the music, his voice quivering high and low as his freshly shaven head wiggled up and down.

A khaki-colored army truck with a big red cross on the hood came to get our instruments and costumes next day. Mr. Fukui and Hideyo went with the truck, and Mother, Ko, and I followed in a taxi amid clouds of dust.

The military base was off-limits to civilians and I was curious. We were halted at a gate by army police, then waved on. We came to a huge white building where Major Ryu, an army doctor, greeted us. He said all of the wounded soldiers had been looking forward to this day.

There were other children backstage in a giant auditorium, here to show their talents in singing, poetry reading, and *koto* playing.

While I was changing into my *kimono* costume I began to hear people entering the auditorium, and I peeked through the heavy curtains. Wounded soldiers, wearing white hospital gowns, came streaming in. Some wore slings, some walked with crutches, some, their eyes bandaged, were led by nurses. Some had no arm, or no leg, and what shocked me most was a man on a stretcher who had no arms or legs. I pulled Mother's kimono sleeve, wanting her to look. She said she couldn't, her heart ached.

Suddenly I began to feel very nervous. "I don't want to dance," I whispered. My lips were dry from seeing all those wounded.

"Are you nervous about making mistakes?" Mother asked.

I shook my head. "A soldier out there has no arms or legs."

"That is why you are here—to give them a little happiness."

The stiff, high-ranking officers marched in and took side seats. The doctors and nurses took their seats. Major Ryu stood on the stage and announced that the gifted children of this town had come to give a performance.

The program began. Between the performances of other children, singing and playing the koto, I danced. I was the littlest in the whole group, so when I came on the stage and bowed there were yells. "How old are you?" "Do you still wear diapers?"

Everyone burst out laughing, and even serious Mr. Fukui, who was on the stage ready to sing with the *shamisen* so that I could begin, put his hand over his mouth. I felt better and decided to dance my very best to make them all happy.

But I was glad when it was over, and hungry. I wanted to go home. I was taking my *tabi* (socks) off when Major Ryu hurried in. Would we, he begged, come and see some badly wounded soldiers? "We connected speakers to the rooms," he said, "but it would be very nice if you could show yourselves in costume."

We made the rounds. Ko was sweet to everyone, shaking hands and wishing a speedy recovery. "Aren't you scared to touch the wounded soldiers?" I whispered.

"No!" she said. "They fought for our country."

I didn't see any rooms ahead so I thought we could go home. But— "One more," said the doctor. "He is a very difficult patient. He refuses to eat. His recovery would be much faster if he would eat and let us treat him."

"I don't want to," I said. "It makes me feel too sad."

"I know," said the doctor. "But please, one more."

The card on the door said "Corporal Matsumura." I was told to knock and I knocked timidly, but it took considerable persuasion from the doctor before a weak voice said, "Come in."

What I saw chilled me. Corporal Matsumura's entire head and face were bandaged heavily. There were holes for ears, mouth, and the tip of his nose. His eyes were covered. He looked like a mummy.

The doctor explained that we had just performed. He introduced Mother and Ko. "And this is Miss Yoko. She is a very little girl."

I wanted to say "Good day," but my mouth was trembling. I bowed.

"Miss Yoko bowed to you, Corporal," said the doctor.

The Corporal brought his right arm from under the sheet. His arms were bandaged but not his hands. I did not want to shake hands with him, but Ko put my hand in his. His soft, warm, huge hand fingered mine. "How old are you?"

"I . . . I . . . I'm almost twelve, sir."

"So tiny, this hand. Like a miniature maple leaf," he murmured.

There was silence. I felt very uncomfortable. Then, gently, the Corporal's hand moved up my shoulder and touched my forehead. He found a small scar. "Where did you get this?"

"I . . . I fought with boys, sir."

I could almost see a smile. "Did you win?"

"No, sir."

The smile seemed a little broader. Now his fingers examined the material of my costume. He touched my *obi,* the sash. "What a beautiful costume you are wearing," he said. "I wish I could have seen you dance in this costume."

I did not know what to say.

"You take dance lessons?" he asked. Twice a week, I told him.

"When these doctors release me, may I come and see you dance?"

Mother nodded at me and I said, "Ye—yes. Please."

Then he asked about my name. "There are lots of characters for 'Yoko.' How do you write your Yoko?"

Ko poked me and her lips said, "Answer!"

"My name Yoko means to protect or to embrace, sir."

"That is a difficult character," he said. "Will you show me how to write your name when I visit you?"

This time Mother and Ko were both nodding. "P-p-please," I said.

Then Ko, Mother, and Mr. Fukui wished the Corporal a speedy recovery and we left, to my great relief. How could I know this man was to be important in my life?

A few weeks later, in May, we were having dinner and I had been complaining about the cooked carrots and *tofu* that we had had for three days straight. Not only rice, but vegetables and fish were rationed, and Mother added oats, barley, or vegetables when she cooked rice. Every time she was able to get fish she cooked it, dried it, and packed it in our emergency kits. Although I did not like rice cooked with oats or barley, I ate that. But plain carrots . . .

"Don't complain, Little One," Hideyo scolded me. "You should be glad there is food on your plate."

"I don't like carrots. Cooked or uncooked."

"Stupid One. Someday you'll wish you had these." And he reached over with his chopsticks and picked up all the carrots.

Someone called, "Good evening."

"Yes, right away," Mother replied. I was surprised when she returned with Corporal Matsumura. By chance, he had come on the day of my dancing lesson. He was wearing a hospital gown of white canvaslike material in kimono style and his face was uncovered. It was disfigured and the scars looked fresh and painful.

He ate the supper that Mother brought to him on a small vermilion-lacquered table, and drank the tea Ko poured. "You've made a fantastic recovery, Corporal," Hideyo told him. Hideyo was acting the role of Father.

"Meeting your sisters made me want to get well," the Corporal said.

Mr. Fukui came and tuned our shamisen. I bowed deeply to him and began my lesson, doing my very best this time, for our special guest.

Corporal Matsumura visited often and we grew to like him very much. We relaxed when he came and listened with interest to what he told us of his hometown in Japan. He was knowledgeable in classical poetry and had translated many poems into modern Japanese.

Summer warmed the night air, but the city hall ordered us to drape all windows with dark and heavy cloth, so that enemy planes could not spot the least light. Ko helped Mother make drapes. She was good at sewing and taught me how to make simple nightclothes as consolation gifts for battlefield soldiers. I made two of the garments. When I wrapped them, I slipped a letter in the pocket that gave all the news of our town and ended with, "When you happen to invade a village, please do not kill or beat women, children, and aged." When I wrote the last sentence, I thought of the mean army police who had recently come, and automatically put my hand over my side.

Now day after day we heard the air raid siren. If

we were at home, we rushed to the shelter, grabbing our emergency bags. If the air raid came while we were laboring outside, we flattened ourselves on the ground. The American bombers always flew in formation. Mr. Enomoto said they looked like B-29s, the same model that had been attacking Tokyo and major cities in the homeland. Every time they flew over, I was scared that this town would also turn to waves of fire and we would be burned to death.

And night after night the alert siren woke us. Because it was dark inside and out, the night air raids seemed more eerie. The night planes flew very low. They shook the whole earth. I could hear bamboo, bent almost double, making cracking noises. Everyone lost sleep and everyone looked very tired the next day.

One night Hideyo told Mother he had made a decision: to join *Yokaren*, the student army.

"What?" Ko shouted. Mother opened her mouth and could not close it for several seconds.

"Most of my classmates have enlisted," said Hideyo, serious for once. "I have decided to go to help our country."

"You cannot go, Hideyo!" Mother told him. "You must talk with Father. You just cannot make such a decision alone."

"Mother, I have already sent in my application," said Hideyo. "I will take the written and physical examinations!"

"How could you?" Mother moaned. "Why didn't you tell me?"

"I am eighteen. Big enough to make my own decision."

"Eighteen or nineteen, even twenty-one, doesn't make a difference. Wait until Father comes home!"

"Not that I am disrespectful to you, Mother, but

you don't understand what's going on in the world," said Hideyo. "Our country needs young soldiers."

Mother became more angry. "This Tojo government attacking Pearl Harbor to start the war was bad enough. Your father disagrees with the Japanese government." Mother's voice began to shake. "The government has been taking away everything we have—peace, love, happiness. I would rather see our country lose the war than lose my husband and son!" She burst into tears.

Hideyo left the room and Ko quickly cleared the table. I did not know how to comfort Mother, so I left her.

Mother and Hideyo argued day after day. She wired Father to come home, but he wired back that he was attending an important meeting with other government officials.

By now Mother and Hideyo were no longer speaking. Ko decided to do something. She went to Hideyo's room and I went too.

"At least you can speak to your mother, Honorable Brother," said Ko.

"Leave me alone!" Hideyo snapped. "Stupid girls. You don't understand a thing. Go away!"

"I will not go away until I say my piece," Ko said bluntly.

"Then say it and get out!"

Ko told Hideyo that he must not join Yokaren because if Father died, who would look after Mother and his sisters? Who would carry on the family name?

"Mother would adopt a son," said Hideyo coldly.

"You may think joining the student army and dying for the country would be glorious and make you a hero," Ko went on. "And the government would send Mother a distinguished medal for your courageous death. Do you think Mother would want it? No!"

"There are only old and feeble men in the war zone now," said Hideyo. "The healthy ones have been either killed or wounded. Also, I cannot go to school every day peacefully while my classmates are getting killed. I have thought about this for a long time."

"Listen." Ko's tone was even more emphatic. "Today while I was laboring at the parade ground I saw a bunch of half-recovered soldiers in their hospital gowns. They were being trained to carry food in the war zone under simulated fire and bombing. I spotted Corporal Matsumura. All of them looked dragged out. I thought, if our country is gathering up young ones and forcing still-wounded soldiers back to the battlefield, well, there is no hope of winning this war. You are wasting your life." She shouted, "If you join the army I disown you as an honorable brother and I will not speak to you as long as I live!"

"Me too!" I said. "Ever!"

"I won't let girls tell me what to do! Now get out!" Hideyo shouted. But as he banged the door, he called, "I'll handle it!"

A few weeks later a special delivery letter came from army headquarters. It was addressed to Father, so Hideyo, who was head of the house in Father's absence, should have opened it. But he had gone to the training ground.

So Mother opened it. It was the result of Hideyo's written and physical tests, and Ko and I gathered around to see what the letter said. Mother's hand shook, her face was very pale. My heart thumped.

Then her expression changed to relief. "What does it say, Mother?" Ko asked eagerly.

For the first time in many days Mother really

smiled. "Look!" She showed us the letter. "Hideyo passed the physical but failed the written test. They say he is not bright enough for Japan's Imperial Army, so they are putting him to work in an ammunition factory, six days a week, in a town twenty miles from here."

"What do you mean, Honorable Brother is not bright?" Ko demanded. We put our heads over the examination papers enclosed. Suddenly Ko burst out laughing.

"Sure, sure! Honorable Brother is very stupid in the eyes of the examiners. Look at this! Your son deliberately put down the wrong answers. These are questions even our Little One can answer!"

The day came when Hideyo had to go to the factory. Mother packed food and clothes in his huge rucksack and told him she had included needles and thread. Hideyo put on his heavy boots and khaki leg wrappers.

"Well, see you in six days," he said. Then in a really serious tone he told Ko, "Look after Mother and Little One."

Ko nodded, with a big smile. I smiled too, because I wanted him to work in the factory rather than join the army and get killed.

We all walked beyond the bamboo grove to see him off, and the three of us stood there, very still, until he made the turn toward the station.

The house seemed empty that night. None of us spoke as we ate supper. Then Mother broke the silence. "Father wrote. He asked if our emergency bags were ready. He said, even though it's summer, we should take some winter clothes to the shelter with us . . . just in case we must evacuate."

In the dim light I started my composition homework. I titled the composition "Grandparents."

As I wrote, my thoughts drifted and I wondered when I would meet mine. I looked at the paper, but I could not even read my writing in this light. I gave a deep sigh. *When will peace come so we can turn on the lights?* I heard the last train pass. It was bedtime. I was so tired I threw myself down on top of the *futon* with my clothes on, hoping there would be no air raid to wake me.

Suddenly I was startled awake by someone pounding and calling.

Half asleep, I got up. At the front entrance Mother, holding a candle, was arguing with someone. Ko joined her. Then Ko saw me. "It's Corporal Matsumura. He tells us to get out fast!"

"No! Corporal, I cannot leave now!" Mother was saying. "Hideyo won't be back until Saturday. I cannot leave without him!"

"I came as fast as I could to warn you," the Corporal told her. "The Russians are landing. They will be looking especially for you and your family. They will kill you."

"Why?"

"Because of your husband's work for Japanese interests in Manchuria."

"How can I go without my son?"

"Leave a note telling him to meet you at Seoul, at the train station." The Corporal spoke hurriedly. "A hospital train is evacuating Japanese patients and they leave at four a.m. I arranged with the stationmaster for you to get on. He is my friend." He fumbled in his pocket. "This is a note to the stationmaster. Go now!"

Mother was speechless. Still not fully awake, I sensed something awful was happening.

Corporal Matsumura looked at me. In the candlelight his scarred face turned red and frightening. He took hold of my chin and smiled. Then he touched his lips to my forehead. "I will not forget you," he said. And to Mother, "I have been assigned to the war zone again—I don't know where. I appreciate your friendship very much." He bowed deeply.

Just as he was leaving I stopped him. I ran to my room and grabbed my calligraphy—*"Bu Un Cho Kyu"* (Good Luck in War). I rolled it quickly and rushed back. "Please take this."

The Corporal unrolled it and Mother moved the candle nearer so he could read. "Thank you very much. I wish you good luck too!" And he faded into the darkness.

"Mother," said Ko, "you and Little One leave. I'll stay behind and wait for Honorable Brother."

"No, we shall all leave together." Mother was definite now though her voice shook. "You leave a note for Father, Ko, and I will write one for Hideyo. Little One, put your winter coat on."

"What? A winter coat?" I was so tired and sleepy that I was in an ugly mood.

"Obey me!" Mother's voice commanded. "And fill all our canteens with water. Do you hear me?" She had never spoken to me so harshly.

I went back to my room. Ko was writing a note to Father in the dim light. I gathered my composition papers and pencils.

"You have no time for that!" Ko screamed at me. "Hurry up and fill the canteens!"

I dragged six canteens toward the kitchen. My head was dizzy and I staggered. Ko yanked the canteens from me and rushed to the kitchen pump. I tried to walk toward the entrance to grab my emergency bag, but I seemed to be on a boat on an angry sea.

Ko grabbed my hand and pulled me to the entrance, where Mother stood, already carrying her large wrapping cloth pack on her back.

Chapter 2

We took the road along the river, the shortest way to the station. There were many large potholes, and when I stumbled I felt the strong tug of Mother's rope on my wrist. The rough rope rubbed and hurt me. My stomach was churning with fright.

"I don't feel good." I was half crying.

"*Shh!*" Mother stood still. "I hear something," she whispered.

We listened. In the distance was the sound of marching feet.

"Have the Russians landed now?" Mother asked.

"Hide in the wild irises," Ko ordered, and we slid down the steep riverbank over scratchy weeds and small stones.

The marching grew louder. I flattened myself on the bank. Mother slid her pack to the ground and lay beside me. Ko raised her head. "They're coming toward the river."

I moved toward Mother and she put her arm around me and pulled me close. My heart was thumping.

I heard a man's shout. The swift-running river drowned his words, but then they came nearer. "One, two, three, four!" The vigorous voice was shouting in the Korean language. "One, two, three, four!"

They were close to us. I did not dare move an inch.

"They must be Koreans, from the Anti-Japanese Communist Army," Ko whispered.

The voice was shouting again. "Stop! All run to the river field. We are about to practice killing our enemies!"

They mean us, I thought, the Japanese.

There was the thudding of feet as the troop ran down the bank. I could not stop shaking, and Mother's arms, holding me tightly, trembled.

Very close to us the troop commander was explaining how to stab "the enemies" and how to defend themselves. And how to drag bodies into the river or into trenches.

Suddenly I vomited. Quickly Ko threw herself over my head so that the troop, so close, would not hear me. Again and again I gagged, and each time Ko pressed her body on my head.

A whistle shrieked. There was silence. Then I heard a voice commanding, "Swim the river!"

Our breath held, we listened as the marching steps and the "One, two, three, four" faded into the distance. I was weak with relief.

Mother took my rucksack and the canteens. She drew me to the river and whispered to me to wash my mouth and face.

Ko put Mother's bundle on her own back. It was much too heavy, she said. Mother could carry Ko's rucksack. And once more we were on the road, Mother pulling the rope. "We must hurry," she whispered.

I felt somewhat better now but I began to shiver. I whined. "I want Honorable Father!"

"Walk!" said Ko.

Normally I could walk to the station in forty minutes by this road, and I always met Father when he came home, but now it seemed as if I had been walking for hours. I prayed that there would be no air raid or other danger to flatten me on the ground. When at last I saw a faint light in the distance I asked Ko, "Is that the station?"

"Right," said Ko. "Don't talk. Just walk."

Ko is bossy, I thought. But the light ahead gave me comfort. Maybe I could rest when I got there. I forced myself to a faster walk.

When we came in sight of the station, flooded with light, the scene shocked me awake. Hospital trucks and army trucks jammed the grounds. Everywhere were soldiers and civilian medical teams carrying wounded soldiers on stretchers onto the platform. Other wounded were walking with crutches. Some were being led by nurses. Everywhere there was hustling, running, scurrying here and there to assist patients, adults and children.

Mother tugged and we moved to the platform. She needed to find the stationmaster, but I had eyes only for the nightmarish scene, with two engines spitting steam and smoke. They looked ready to depart. Would they leave us? Would we get on? Behind the two engines stretched boxcars as far as I could see.

The medical team was carrying patients into the boxcars. People were screaming. A voice begged someone to look for someone. A pregnant woman, crying, bowed to her husband, and a pale woman in soft nightclothes, holding her baby in her arms, sobbed as a man—her husband, I assumed—peeked at the baby and talked to her. She kept nodding. As we came near to them I heard him say to her, "Take good care of your life. I shall look after everything."

Mother could not find the stationmaster. She asked a worker where he was but he did not know. She was still pulling our ropes as she made her way among the patients. Our sacks bumped people and people bumped us. A stretcher handle hit my ribs where the police had kicked me and I cried out with pain.

We went to the stationmaster's room, but he was not there. Mother looked in the waiting room, also jammed with patients. One man was spitting blood.

Some had fainted and were lying on the floor. Children cried. An old woman screamed and pulled at her gray hair. Amidst all of this the medics checked patients' names and nodded to the stretcher bearers. Then the patients were carried out to the boxcars.

"Where is the stationmaster?" Mother asked a medic in desperation.

"Out there."

We found him, and he was talking to the army doctor, Major Ryu. The Major recognized us and we exchanged greetings. "I have permission to board the train," said Mother.

The Korean stationmaster looked us over. I trembled at the coldness in his eyes. "You don't look sick," he said. "The train is for patients only."

"Corporal Matsumura said he made an arrangement with you."

"Corporal who?"

There was such screaming and yelling that the stationmaster could not hear Mother.

"Corporal Matsumura! He said you are his friend."

The man looked at us. We were not going to make it. My stomach was misbehaving again.

"Let them get on!" said the doctor. "I know this family."

Then Mother remembered the note. She took it from her pocket and thrust it at the stationmaster, her hand shaking.

He read it. "Madame Kawashima, son Hideyo, daughters Ko and Yoko. Where is your son?"

"He left this morning for the ammunition factory where he will work with the mobilized students."

Major Ryu spoke to the stationmaster now in a tone of authority.

"Put them on the train. This is my order. Mrs.

Kawashima indeed has a son. He was at the army hospital with them."

And at last the stationmaster gave in. "All right, you get on the women's boxcar." His voice was tired now.

I heard Ko's deep sigh. Mother bowed to Major Ryu and Ko and I did too, because he had rescued us.

By the time we found the women's boxcar there were fewer people on the platform. Mother finally untied our wrists. Ko dropped her bundle on the platform, put both hands on the edge of the boxcar and pushed herself up. Mother handed her the bundle and then she told me to get on. But no matter how high I stretched and jumped I could not reach the edge of the car. Finally I held up my arms and Ko pulled. I thought my arms would be pulled off my shoulders. Mother grabbed my legs and pushed, but the canteens I carried on both shoulders jammed against the edge of the car. Ko had to let go and Mother made me drop the rucksack and canteens on the platform. Then, pulled and pushed once more, I finally rolled into the boxcar.

Mother tossed my belongings, also her own, to Ko. Then she put both hands on the edge of the car and jumped, but failed.

The train whistled three times. Frantically I pulled at Mother's arm but she was too heavy. She tried again and made it to her chest. She was wriggling desperately to get in, when a medic and a nurse came by—and they pushed Mother into the car.

We were aboard. Safe. I looked around. The boxcar was dark, without any light, and it smelled of machine oil. I could not see the patients' faces, but my eyes gradually became used to the darkness and I saw that the people were symmetrically arranged on cheaply woven straw mats. There was almost no space between patients.

I squeezed myself between the woman and new baby and the pregnant woman, folding my knees toward my chest. An aged woman stared into space, her mouth open. Some groaned in pain, some were crying for help. A woman's hand waved in the air, wanting to hold onto someone. Mother reached out her hand and the woman gripped it.

The pregnant woman was calling for water. I opened my canteen and gave her a capful. "Don't waste your water," Ko whispered.

"But she was thirsty."

"You'll be thirsty yourself," said Ko without emotion.

The train whistled once. I heard steam puffing. Then a female nurse and a male medic hopped onto the car, and the medic fastened a fat rope across the door. He stretched his body outward and waved his hand. The train whistled once more. There was a commotion outside. Someone was shouting and asking if there was any room in our boxcar. "There are a few more patients," a voice called.

The medic shouted, "We can take three more." And three women were put on board, two on stretchers, one with her head bandaged. When they were on, the train moved, slowly.

The nurse made an announcement. There were two large wooden tubs in the corner, she said, one for urine, one for bowel movements. In another corner were stacked boxes of items for medical care.

The train increased its speed. The wind was blowing in strongly now, and the sky began to show pale pink. "We're coming back home soon, aren't we?" I asked Mother, so anxiously.

She nodded reassurance. This would be just temporary.

Ko went to the door and held on to the rope at the opening. The medic ordered her to stay away, as it was dangerous, but I heard her tell him she wanted to see our house. Then I got up and went to the opening too. I held on to Ko, as the wind was strong enough to blow me away. Over the wind Ko told me that we would pass our house very soon. I stretched my neck to the left.

"There is the house!" Ko cried, and I saw faintly the dark red tiles of our roof. It came nearer, nearer. I saw the top of the old familiar willow tree, with the tall bamboo pole for our radio antenna. I remembered Father and Hideyo working on it one summer. House and willow looked very sleepy in the early morning air.

The train passed by them. I twisted my head far to the right to watch. The red roof, the willow tree, the radio antenna drew farther away. Soon they were out of my sight. I returned to my place.

Mother was crying, her handkerchief over her eyes. She did not want to see what Ko and I saw.

The nurse and the medic were checking on the patients. When the medic came to Mother she asked his age. "Twenty-one," he said. Her tears came again and she told him softly that she had a son near his age. At this mention of Hideyo my own tears came, thinking of Honorable Brother going home to an empty house.

The train jolted on toward the south. When the pregnant woman asked for water I gave her another tiny capful from my canteen. Ko talked to all of the patients, sometimes wiping their faces.

Somehow that day passed. When evening came I was hungry. I had eaten nothing since leaving home. I fumbled through my sack but Mother stopped me. The others too had not eaten in all that time, and it would not be fair to them if I ate.

The dark enveloped the train. I could not see the flying scenes from the opening. I put my sack between my legs and rested my head on it to catch a little sleep, but sleep was disturbed by the wind and the moaning of the patients.

I was glad when morning came again. I asked Mother if I could eat something, but she shook her head.

"But I'm starved," I whispered.

"Everyone is hungry," she said. "We don't have enough food to go around. We'll be arriving in Seoul tomorrow and then we will cook something. Drink a little water."

The train whistled three times, warning that we were about to enter a tunnel. Then we were wrapped in complete darkness and smoke. Sparks flew in and landed on my bare arms and neck. I could not breathe. My body seemed pricked by thousands of needles from all directions. I coughed and the more I coughed the more smoke entered my throat. My chest was stinging. I held my breath. I opened my mouth a little to breathe. Now I was very dizzy and wondered if I was going to die. I called to Ko and she put her blanket over me and pushed my head to the floor. Then I fainted.

The next I knew, the nurse was slapping my face. We were out of the tunnel. Mother was there, her face streaked with soot. Ko's face looked the same.

"Feel better now?" asked Ko.

"My throat burns and my chest stings," I murmured.

"Suck on this." Ko put something in my palm.

"Where did you get caramels?" I whispered in wonder.

"I am a great magician." Ko smiled.

The woman who had just had her baby sat up, holding her child, and brought out her milk-filled breast. "You have been such a good baby," she said proudly. "You must be very hungry." She brought her nipple to the baby's mouth. The baby was sound asleep.

"Wake up, Toshi-chan. It's your feeding time." So I knew the baby was a manchild. The baby's eyes and mouth stayed tightly closed. She shook the child frantically and the tiny head flopped up and down. "Wake up!" the woman screamed.

The medic and the nurse examined the baby and pronounced him dead. The medic crossed the name from the list he carried and told the woman he would take care of the body. I wondered how he would take care of the tiny dead baby. He ordered the woman to hand him the child but she screamed her husband's name, begging him for help, telling him the medic had killed their son and was about to throw him away.

Mother touched the woman gently. She glared at Mother for a few moments, then she sobbed. Mother took out her nail scissors and clipped the baby's fingernails. I never knew a baby's fingers were so tiny. She clipped a small lock of the baby's hair, and she wrapped the clippings in tissue paper and handed them to the woman. The woman seemed utterly mad now. She grabbed the tiny parcel and crammed it between her breasts.

The nurse tried to take the dead baby but the mother resisted. Then the medic yanked the baby from her and quickly tossed it from the train. The tiny body floated in the air like a rag doll for a moment and vanished.

The mother's eyes were fixed on the opening. Then she stood, stumbled over me, and, quick as lightning, jumped from the fast-moving train.

A shriek trailed in the air.

"Ah!" Mother buried her head in her arms.

The nurse began checking the patients. She put her stethoscope on their chests and if there was no heartbeat she lowered the eyelids. She called the dead patients' names clearly, twice, and the medic crossed them off.

Then the medic told Ko and me to get up and make room. The nurse helped him drag the dead to the opening and they rolled the corpses outside. Mother's eyes were closed and the hand over her forehead shook.

There were lots of empty spaces now. I went to the opening, held on to the rope, and looked out. I saw many bodies, tossed out of other cars, rolling down the bank to the fields.

The nurse announced that she and the medic were about to give everyone a shot on the thigh. There was no food and the shot would give nourishment. I asked the nurse if she was going to give me one.

"No," she said. "You are healthy."

Hunger was a pain in my stomach. I asked Mother if I could eat a little piece of dried fish. "I'll die otherwise!"

She nodded. When Ko saw me opening my sack she opened hers. She tore the dried fish in small pieces and shared hers with Mother.

As I was chewing, the pregnant woman stared. I said, "Are you hungry?" She nodded weakly. I stripped the fish into small pieces, removed the bones carefully, and gave her some. I chewed even the bones, until they were soft, then swallowed them.

Everyone wanted water. My canteen was empty. Mother poured a few drops on a washrag and let some patients suck. One woman crawled to the urine tub, put her hand in and sucked it.

I was exhausted. I had not lain down since we got on the train, but now there was space for me to stretch. How good it felt to lie down. I decided to sleep.

But the pregnant woman next to me began moaning. I changed my position. Her screams came periodically. I sat up.

"Lie down," Mother told me. "Pay no attention. Go to sleep." I lay down again.

Suddenly I felt wet warmth on my back. I whispered to Mother that the woman had wet her pants. Mother seemed about to tell me something but changed her mind. I shifted my position, and there was another scream.

I knew the medic and nurse were at the woman's side. The screams were so terrible that I thought they must be operating on her without a painkiller. Again I felt something warm on my shoulders, and this time it was blood, seeping through the cheap mat. Another scream. The nurse was encouraging the woman to scream, and to push. Then suddenly a baby's cry burst out.

I sat up, very uncomfortable in the wet blouse, and decided to change my clothes. "Not now," Mother said. "When we reach Seoul we'll find a public bath house."

All our canteens were empty now, so there was no water at all. The nurse carried the tiny manchild to the tub and washed it with urine. Then she found little clothes among the mother's belongings, dressed the baby, and put him into his mother's arms. Exhausted, the woman smiled weakly at her son, and they both went to sleep.

The sun was almost down now and the air cold. "Put your blanket over the new mother and her baby," Mother said.

"No!" I protested. "I don't want my blanket stained with blood."

"Yoko!" When Mother called me by my name she was angry with me. "Ko is sharing hers with another patient. That new mother will be shivering. Cover her! Now!"

I put my fleecy blanket over the woman and baby, and the new mother opened her eyes. "Thank you," she said in a faint voice. "I was cold."

The train's speed was lessening, and soon we came to a halt. Oh, were we in Seoul? I was already picking up my coat and pulling the blanket from the woman and baby. The medic was holding on to the rope and leaning out. "Is this Seoul?" I asked.

He did not reply at once. Then he drew his head in, saw me, and gave me a look that frightened me. "Go back and lie down immediately!" he said. He spoke to the nurse. "The Korean Communist Army is inspecting the cars!"

He threw me, roughly, to the bloodstained floor, grabbed Ko, and ordered her to lie down. The nurse ran to the urine tub, picked up the placenta, dripping with urine, put it on Ko's abdomen, and told her, "Don't move!" She covered Ko with a large sheet.

Mother was confused and asked the medic what was happening. "We may have trouble," he said, and told her to lie down too.

The nurse and medic were doing crazy things. They took off my bloodstained blouse and rubbed it against Mother's and Ko's faces. The nurse undid Mother's hair and spread it against the mat. She told me to put my stained blouse back on and lie down. The medic was looking out through the opening.

"Where is this?" Mother whispered to the nurse.

"Wŏnsan. We stopped for coal and water, which

they'll give us because this is a hospital train. But the Communists are getting on." She leaned over Mother to whisper, "You have helped us. Don't worry, we will help you."

"Here they come," the medic called softly. "Keep still!"

I heard loud voices, and two Korean men, wearing Korean Communist uniforms, jumped into the car.

"Are these all sick people?" one asked in poor Japanese.

"Right," answered the medic.

"We are looking for healthy Japanese. A middle-aged woman with two girls, about sixteen and eight, and a boy, nineteen, got on at Nanam. The name is Kawashima."

The medic did not look toward us. "There are no such people here. These are all women and children."

"Let me see the hospital list," the voice ordered.

The other Korean Communist soldier was walking among the patients, poking at them with the tip of his gun. My teeth were chattering, my heart thumping. The soldier poked my side. "How old is she?"

"Six," answered the nurse. "Her back is badly wounded."

I was opening my mouth to say I was not six when something warned me for once in my life to keep my mouth shut.

He paused beside Ko, under the sheet, and asked if she was about to have a baby.

"Any moment," said the nurse.

"How old is she?"

"Twenty-two."

"What is the matter with this old woman?" That was Mother.

"She has smallpox. Stay away from her!"

They jumped off our car in a hurry then, and I

could hear them scrambling into the next car. Searching for Mother, Ko, and me.

The medic whispered that we were not to stir an inch until the train was moving again. Mother asked if he could fill our canteens. He did and gave water to each of the patients.

"Oh!" Ko murmured. "How sweet this water is!"

The nurse emptied and cleaned the two toilet tubs.

What a relief when the train began moving again. I got up and looked at the tiny baby. He was wiggling and began crying. The new mother was trying to nurse him but she had no milk, probably, Mother said, because of worry and fear. The baby was crying like mad.

He sucked his mother's nipple a few times and let out another hungry yell. She had no baby bottle so the new mother took a mouthful of water and transferred it into her son's tiny mouth.

The night advanced. The cruel, arrogant air blew in. I put my coat on and lent my blanket again to the new mother and baby. I lay down, to try and get some sleep and shorten the time to Seoul.

The train stopped with a sudden jerk.

Booooom! Waaaam! Airplanes flew over us. *Booooom!*

The medic looked out. "The first engine got hit!" he shouted. *Waaaam*, another plane. *Booooom*, another explosion. The train shook.

The nurse looked out. "Oh, God, the second engine was hit!"

Ko and I went to look out. There was a roar of fire from our two engines. All the medics and nurses were jumping off their assigned cars and running toward the front. I could see their figures clearly in the bright light from the roaring fire.

Quickly they began to evacuate patients in the first

few cars. They were bringing them toward us on stretchers. Some patients were running with the nurses to safe spots.

Mother said she would go and help and Ko said she would go too. They jumped gallantly from the car.

"I want to go," I said.

"No, you stay," Ko told me. "The patients may need your help."

I looked around me. All those sick people looked pale as ghosts in the oily, smelly, dark freight car. Someone began to sob. I felt terribly alone, wishing that Ko or Mother would hurry back.

The medics and nurses brought patients into our car. Ko and Mother led some who could walk. Before long the car was full, and this time men patients had joined us.

When the transfer was finished, our medic and nurse returned. They told Mother that the Red Cross had wired ahead for another engine, but there was no telling when it would come.

"They were not supposed to attack a hospital train or ship. That's the law," said the medic, frustrated.

"Where are we now?" asked Mother.

"About forty-five miles from Seoul."

"How dangerous would it be if we walked?"

"Maybe safer than staying with us," the medic said. "Someone may betray you here."

"Just follow the rails to the south," the nurse said.

We said farewell to the patients in the boxcar. I left all my dried fish, hard biscuits, and dried radishes for the new mother, and Ko left her one of the canteens filled with water, saying she needed nourishment.

The new mother, her baby crying, held my hand and would not let it go. "Thank you!" she said.

"Take care of your baby," said Mother.

The new mother nodded, in tears.

Ko jumped off first. Mother dropped her large pack on the ground and jumped with the help of the medic. I dropped Ko's and my sacks and our canteens. The medic stretched his arms up. As I stood at the edge of the car I realized how high up from the ground I was.

"Jump!" shouted Ko, already putting Mother's large wrapping cloth bundle on her back.

I closed my eyes and leaned forward, hoping I would not fall flat on my face and break my nose. My stomach tickled and I landed safely in the arms of the medic.

Mother asked the nurse what time it was. It was three a.m. We bowed deeply to the medic and nurse, our sincere thanks.

The burning engines gave tremendous heat as we walked by, their thick iron frames turned red as if to melt at any moment. Through an opening I saw the body of an engineer, burnt black. "Don't look," Ko said. Mother kept on walking.

We had been the only healthy ones to get on the train at Nanam, and now we were the only healthy ones to get off. I looked at the long road we were about to take, rails stretching ahead, shining mysteriously in the light of a three-quarter moon.

Ko yanked my hand to keep pace with Mother toward Seoul.

Chapter 3

We walked until daylight broke in the sky. Mother said we must find some thicket off the track and get some sleep and hide during the day to avoid being captured. By the time we found large bushes, we were completely exhausted. We crawled into them and slept, covered with our blankets.

I woke, feeling terribly hot, and kicked off my blanket. At first I did not know where I was. Then I realized I was sleeping in the thicket. The sun was shining brightly. I was thirsty, and I opened my canteen and drank a small capful of water. Again I drank. I looked inside the sack for something to eat, then I realized I had given all my food supplies to the new mother and baby. I reached to Ko's rucksack and she woke.

"I'm hungry," I said.

"Let's cook some rice," said Ko. "Go gather some wood."

She opened her sack and took out her mess kit. She measured half a cup of rice and used the rest of my canteen water to cook it over a fire she built between small rocks. For the first time in four days we ate small portions of fluffy rice, with small pieces of dried fish from Mother's kit. I was still hungry, but Ko said we must use the rice sparingly, as we did not know what might lie ahead. We stayed there until twilight wrapped us in darkness. Then again we were on the railroad track.

Sometimes we heard strange noises and feared they came from soldiers. We would quickly run from the main track. With my rucksack and canteens bouncing about me, I would stumble in holes and on weed-mounds. Mother would grab my arm to help me get up, pulling me along strongly until I could run no longer. My face, scratched from falling, kept bleeding. Often when we were off the main track, we got lost. It was Ko who always scouted ahead to find the right path.

For seven nights we followed the tracks. No train went by, not even a hospital train. As each morning came we searched for a thicket, and when night came we kept on our journey.

My legs became numb. I whined, "I can't walk anymore."

"You've got to," Ko said bluntly. "Don't talk, just walk!" She was getting very bossy.

On the eighth night we came to an iron railroad bridge. As I stood looking down at the water beneath, that bridge seemed a hundred times higher than the edge of the boxcar. Far, far below me the torrents of water made a roaring sound.

We stood still. I could not cross that high bridge on the railroad ties in the night with only the moon for light. Ko suddenly lay down on the ground and put her ear to the rail. She kept that position for a long time, listening.

"What are you doing?" asked Mother.

"Listening for vibrations," Ko said. "For a train. No train is coming. We must cross this bridge."

I was already dizzy. I looked at the ties and saw how far apart they were. "I'll fall through into the river," I said. "Let's swim it."

Ko said no. She and I were good swimmers, but the current was too strong. Besides, Mother could not swim.

"But a train might come," I argued.

"A train won't come if we cross quickly. And

tomorrow night there will be less moonlight to see by. Come!"

Ko went ahead of us. She walked on the ties as easily as if they were a smooth road. I held onto Mother's hand, knees shaking. When Mother took a step, I took a step. Then another. I tried not to see the roaring water below. But if I did not watch where I put my foot, I could fall through the ties. And maybe, I thought, my canteen and rucksack would be stuck and there I would hang beneath the ties.

Ko kept on walking. Once in a while she looked back to see where we were, then she took much faster steps, and she was almost across.

"It's mean of Honorable Sister," I mumbled at Mother. "She is way ahead of us."

"She is a wonderful sister to you," said Mother. "I would not know how to manage without her."

"You're always on her side," I said. "I'm beginning to hate her."

Mother glanced sideways at me and her face was harsh. "How dare you talk like that about your good sister?"

We took another step. And another.

"I am so dizzy," I said. And I stood still and closed my eyes.

"We're halfway across," Mother told me. "Come." But I clung to her, terrified to move lest I tumble through to the river.

And then Ko yelled. "Stay where you are!"

She was hopping back on the ties as easily as if she were jumping rope. She had no pack on her back. When she reached us she turned around, bent over and said to me, "Hop on."

I put myself on her back and locked my arms around her neck.

"Don't choke me, Little One," said Ko, and

coughed. I turned my head toward Mother, and the smile she gave me spoke worlds.

I felt terrible now for saying Ko was a mean sister. I put my head on her shoulder to let her know that I loved her very much.

So we crossed the bridge safely. Mother said now we should wash in the river; we had not bathed since we left home. We searched for a thicket and hid our belongings.

Ko bathed first. She returned to where we were, drying her hair. "Ah, I feel much more alive!"

Mother and I went down to the river. She dipped my head in the water, soaped my hair and rinsed it. She washed my back and I did the same for her. We washed our bloodstained clothes. Upstream Ko filled our canteens.

The bathing refreshed me and now I could have slept, but we had to go on as long as our energy held out, wet clothes flipping and flapping on the back of the rucksacks.

Dawn came and we began hearing airplanes in the distance. We got off the railroad track and hid in a forest. We would stay there during the day, we decided. I was starved but Mother said she was too tired to cook, and it was best anyway not to build a fire while planes were flying over. We decided to sleep.

The airplanes swept above us just as I had fallen off. We went farther into the forest and squeezed into a thicket. There was an explosion in the distance and at the same time the sky turned red.

We had no idea where we were or how far from our destination. But we had found a spot spread with soft moss and Mother decided we should stay there for a real rest.

I slept all day and all night. When the rising sun

sent a soft light between the trees, Ko built a small fire and Mother cooked rice. How I yearned for fresh vegetables and a fine cup of tea. I could even eat carrots; I had refused to all these years. I remembered Hideyo's words vividly. "Someday you'll wish you had these carrots."

When we finished our bits of rice Ko poured a little water into my bowl. She told me to swish it around but not to throw the water away. She dumped the water from my wooden bowl into hers and swished. She passed the water to Mother. Mother sipped a little water, leaving some for Ko and me to drink.

We were putting our cooking utensils away when suddenly, from nowhere, three soldiers in Korean Communist uniforms stood before us. We froze.

"Stand up!" yelled one of the soldiers. He was pointing a machine gun at us. The other two did the same. We stood. I moved closer to Mother.

"Don't move!" they screamed.

My mouth went dry. My knees hardly held me.

"What have you got there?"

"Our belongings," Ko said in the northern Korean accent.

All three soldiers were looking at Ko. "How old are you?"

She did not answer.

"The right size to have fun with tonight," said the first soldier. "Leave all your belo—"

A plane swept above our heads and instantly we three, well trained, flattened ourselves. *Booooom!* An explosion. I seemed to be blowing away, and my head went black.

Someone was shaking me roughly, and I opened my eyes. Mother was saying something that I could not hear. Her hair was smeared with blood and she kept on shaking me like that madwoman in the train. I saw Ko's lips moving.

"I can't hear," I said.

There was a sharp pain in my chest. My hand went there automatically and felt warmth. I looked at my hand. Blood.

I tapped my ears but I was wrapped in complete silence. The soldiers . . . airplanes . . . explosion. I said loudly, "Where are the soldiers?"

Ko's lips formed the word, "Dead." Then she fumbled in my sack and took out paper and pencil.

"Shut up!" she wrote. "We may be discovered by soldiers again. You were not badly wounded. Just a piece of bombshell that burnt your skin. My hearing is not clear either. Yours will come back."

She opened her sack, took out her chemise, and wrapped it around my chest. Mother put my blanket over me and stroked my head, her tears dropping onto my face. I did not bother to wipe them away. I fell off to sleep.

Again I slept all day and all night. I was wakened by Mother early the next morning. Still I could not hear what she said. Both my ears seemed plugged with thick cotton. But I looked at Ko with astonishment. She was wearing a Korean Communist uniform and her thick, long black hair was shaved off. And then I suddenly saw that Mother too was wearing the uniform of a soldier. The dead soldiers', it came to me slowly.

Mother made me sit up, and with her small scissors she cut my hair. "Please, don't shave my head!" I begged.

Ko wrote, "Mother is protecting us from being harmed by soldiers."

When my hair was shortened Ko poured a little water on my head. She soaped it. I fussed and cried and said, "I don't want to be baldheaded!"

"Be still!" Ko wrote. She gave me a look as if to say, "You spoiled brat!"

Mother had brought out from somewhere the family's precious treasure, our ancestors' short sword. Her left hand, holding my head, was trembling. She began shaving. The sharp, thin blade slid over my head and I sobbed. "Where was the sword?" I asked. Mother patted her chest.

Then she said, "Finished," wiped the thin blade carefully, and put it into the sheath. She held the slender sheath out in front of her, and bowed.

Ko put a small mirror in front of me and I adjusted her hand to take a peek. I looked horrible. Ko smiled at me but I gritted my teeth in anger, grabbed an empty canteen, and threw it on the ground as hard as I could.

Mother told me to disguise myself by putting on a dead soldier's uniform. "I am not going to strip clothes from a dead man," I said.

"I already have," said Ko.

She handed me the uniform. It smelled of armpits and smoke, and she helped me put it on. She rolled the sleeves and pants, but it was still much too large.

Very close to us lay the stripped bodies of the three soldiers, who had not flattened themselves on the ground when the bomb burst.

We folded our own clothes, stuffed them into our sacks, cleared everything away, and started to march. "But it's daylight," I protested.

"That's all right. We're wearing Korean uniforms," Ko reminded me.

For a hungry stomach my rucksack was very heavy. With each step the stiff, smelly uniform rubbed against my wounded chest. I said I could not carry my blanket. "It's like iron on my back."

"Give it to me," Ko said. "It's the only bedding you have." She rolled my bloodstained blanket and added it to her own bundle.

We had been walking the tracks for eleven days.

Chapter 4

Hideyo, working with three friends from Nanam, was packing assembled machine guns into thick, metal-lined wooden boxes. He had been at the munitions factory five days.

Now Shoichi straightened and said, "Let's take a break." This meant a trip to the restroom for a cigarette.

Hideyo did not smoke. "Go ahead," he said to Shoichi, Makoto, and Shinzo.

Just as the three disappeared into the restroom Korean Communist soldiers burst into the factory.

There was a terrified rush of workers to cover, though the great factory space offered almost none. Hideyo instinctively dove into the big empty box that lay on its side before him. While hiding in the box, he could look out and see some of the workers. He saw Yasuo, his classmate, grab one of the machine guns, stuff it with bullets—fire.

The soldiers fired back. *Dadadadadadadadada!* Yasuo fell, blood streaming.

Someone at the side threw something heavy—one of the boxes—at the soldiers. Again the enemy machine gun fire. Now there was the sound of people falling all around Hideyo. The blast of the machine guns overpowered his ears. Farther and farther back he squeezed, made himself smaller and smaller, and held his breath.

There was silence. An eerie silence.

"Don't move! We shoot!" The commanding voice spoke in poor Japanese. A Korean, Hideyo thought.

"Line up!" the voice commanded. There were

reluctant footsteps toward the front of the room.

"Hands up!"

Hideyo's heart almost failed. Who had been killed? Who had surrendered? All of those students, many not bright enough to be accepted by Japan's Imperial Army but still a good group, working hard for their country, trying their best to live with humor through the dark days of separation from their families.

And Shoichi, Makoto, and Shinzo, in the restroom. Surely the soldiers would look there. The opening of the box Hideyo was hiding in faced the washroom door. Perhaps they would see him too.

"March! Outside!" The voice was commanding. "We'll get this ammunition after we deliver the prisoners. Check all the bodies. If they are still breathing, shoot!"

"Yes, sir!"

Hideyo edged himself forward. Yasuo's body was so close he could touch it, and he leaned out cautiously and smeared some of the blood streaming from his friend on his own face, his hands, and his clothes. Then he backed into his box.

There was the tramp of feet as soldiers and prisoners left the factory, but other soldiers were moving about. One came so close that all Hideyo saw were his boots. Hideyo closed his eyes, and lay down as if dead.

Dadadadaaaaaa! went a machine gun. Someone had still been alive.

The soldier before Hideyo kicked Yasuo's body. Then he saw Hideyo's arm, and he kicked it. With the tip of his machine gun he poked in at Hideyo's face and side. Hideyo lay as dead.

The man went toward the washroom. Hideyo heard the door kicked open. He held his breath.

"No one in here, sir," the soldier reported. "All the others dead."

"Lock the doors," he was told. "Bring dynamite and blast the building as soon as the ammunition is moved out."

Hideyo heard the commander and the last soldiers leave the room. Still he stayed motionless. The factory door was slammed. Silence.

He waited, staring at Yasuo's body. He heard no sound. Cautiously he crept out from the box and over the body of Yasuo. There were bodies everywhere. Sick, terrified, he crawled among the bodies and the blood, stopping to listen.

He reached the washroom door and pushed with his head to open it. The rusty hinges squeaked.

"Makoto!" Hideyo whispered.

No response.

There were four toilets, all the doors reaching to the floor, all closed. Hideyo stood up.

"Shoichi, Shinzo, Makoto! It's me, Hideyo," he whispered.

The third toilet door opened slightly. Makoto peeked out. "You! Alive!" he gasped. Shoichi and Shinzo came from the same cubicle, shaking, their faces ghostly white.

"We heard the machine guns," said Shinzo, his lips trembling. "We hid together. They never looked. Who got killed?"

"Yasuo was killed right in front of me," Hideyo told them. "I don't know who else. They're going to blow up the building. We have to get out."

Makoto peered cautiously from the window. "They're making the captured ones walk toward the street. They're pointing machine guns at them."

Stealthily they crept to their bunkroom next to the washroom. They crammed belongings into their rucksacks. Then they went back to the washroom and carefully, slowly, so as not to make a sound, they pushed the window open. The soldiers' backs were turned. One by one the boys jumped out and ran around the building toward the mountain.

They had not gone far when they heard the explosion. They turned and watched the factory exploding into the air. Hideyo thought of Yasuo.

"It's almost noon," he said, looking at his watch. "If we take the mountain path now we can be home by early morning."

They began walking. Suddenly Hideyo wondered what had happened to his mother and sisters. He walked faster and faster, the others following.

They walked until they were so weary they had to stop, and Makoto said, "Hey, I'm hungry. Does anyone have any food?"

They all searched their sacks. Mother had packed only six days' rations for Hideyo, as he had expected to go home the next afternoon for the weekend, so he had only some strips of fish and dried biscuits. They sat on the roots of a tree and shared what little he had.

"What time is it?" Makoto asked.

"Five o'clock," Hideyo answered.

"I'm still hungry," said Shinzo.

"Let's look for mushrooms," Makoto suggested.

"Yes! Roasted mushrooms are good!" Shoichi agreed.

Hideyo said, "Look, my friends, let's look for mushrooms as we walk. Every moment is precious."

At dawn they reached Hideyo's home, our home, which stood in its bamboo forest at the edge of the village.

"What the hell!" yelled Hideyo. The main entrance door had been burst open. The service entrance door stood wide. They rushed into the house.

"Mother!" Hideyo called.

Makoto surveyed the desolation before them. "The Korean Communist troops have been here," he said.

"I'm going to my house!" Shinzo cried.

"Let's meet at Shoichi's house later," Hideyo called after them.

He was shocked at the ransacking of his home. He examined the rooms carefully. The hanging scroll painting in the receiving room had been slashed to pieces. Closet doors stood open, their contents pulled out. Fur coats, hats, and his sisters' muffs had been stolen, except for a tiny fur coat lying on the floor.

Little One's, Hideyo thought, and picked it up. Holding it in one arm, he continued to check the rooms. The phonograph-radio was gone. The collection of classical records lay scattered on the floor. Kimono drawers were empty.

He saw the treadle sewing machine. Why had the robbers not taken this? Probably because they did not know how to use it. The machine was covered, as always when not in use, with a black velvet cloth, but a rice bowl sat perched on top. Strange, Hideyo thought. Mother never left anything on top of her machine. He went up to the machine and then he saw Mother's note in script writing beneath the bowl. He read it.

"Honorable Son: We must leave. We shall be waiting for you at the railroad station in Seoul."

The note was dated the day he had left for the factory. And, he observed, it was written in the cursive style, so that no one who did not know calligraphy could read it. He was putting it in his pocket when he saw that Mother's savings book had been with it under the rice bowl. They must have left in haste, he thought, and he took the savings book.

He went to his own room. Whoever had entered here had liked what he possessed. The wall clock, ski shoes, radio, collections of wooden tops he used to play with on the ice, fountain pens, his kimonos as well as formal attire were all gone. His desk drawers had been opened and left in a mess.

In the kitchen he found cookies in the cupboard, and rice in the rice bin. He gathered them all into his rucksack. He stuffed in an aluminum cooking pot, candles, and matches. There was a small barrel next to the rice bin where Mother kept pickled plums, and he put as many into his lunch box as it would hold and wrapped the box in a dish towel. He filled his canteen with water from the kitchen pump.

Then he went back to his own room to gather underwear, socks, and a sweater that had not interested the enemy soldiers. His overcoat was nowhere to be seen. In the bathroom he hastily washed his bloody face. I must go, he was thinking now. They may come back to finish stealing our belongings. He took a bar of soap and a bath towel.

Then he rolled the tiny fur coat in his blanket and tied the blanket on top of his already full rucksack.

Out of habit, he closed and locked the service entrance door. There was no way of locking the main entrance, for it was broken, and he wished he had time to nail a board across the opening.

He headed for the narrow bamboo path when suddenly he turned and ran back to the house. He rushed into the family room and picked up an old family photo album he had remembered seeing. Carrying it under his arm, he left the house behind. He looked at his watch. It was 9:15 a.m.

The sun was above the bamboo trees now, and carrying his heavy bundle made him hotter. He hurried to Shoichi's house, meeting no one on the street and feeling the silence ominous.

Makoto and Shinzo were already at Shoichi's. Makoto was sobbing. Shinzo's and Shoichi's parents had fled south, where their relatives lived, but Makoto's aged parents were dead. An only child, he had no place to go. "Don't you have any relatives at all?" Hideyo asked.

"Not in Korea." Makoto sniffed back tears. "I want to go with you. They are killing Japanese. I am scared."

"You can," said Hideyo. "But we cannot flee from this town in Japanese students' clothes."

They looked at each other. "What are we going to do?" asked Makoto, still crying.

Hideyo snapped his fingers. "I know. Let's go to my family's friends, the Lees. They have been working for my family faithfully for years. Even though they are Koreans, they are not Communists. They'll lend us some clothes."

When they found the bodies of Mr. and Mrs. Lee, beginning to decay in the summer heat, the four students at first were speechless. The stench assailed their nostrils. They had thought Koreans would be safe.

Then Hideyo yelled in anger. "Damn them! My home was ransacked, the valuables were stolen. Now the Communists slaughter good people!" Hideyo sobbed.

"Let's borrow some clothes and get out of here!" yelled Shoichi.

They changed into Korean clothes. They rolled their students' uniforms in their blankets.

There was no map to lead them south, so they decided to follow the railroad tracks. But they had walked all night without sleep, so now they went up on the hill near the Lees' house, crawled into the bushes, and slept until evening came.

Their walking journey began. If they had to speak, they spoke in the Korean language. They slept during the day for fear they would be discovered by the Korean Communist Army. Also, it was cooler to walk through the night.

When they came across vegetable fields they dug up whatever they could find, simply shook the dirt off, and ate the vegetables raw, to save their own food supplies. They sucked the juices from wild plants. They devoured wild carrots and any tomatoes they found, for the heat made them thirsty. They had been walking now for ten days.

Their canteens were empty of water, their lips peeling. When they saw anything green they put it in their mouths and sucked as hard as they could to draw at least a drop of juice. They were exhausted.

"There is a pond!" Hideyo shouted.

Water! They were overjoyed. Hurriedly they walked toward the pond, but the pond was not there. It was a large bloodstain on the ground, and dead bodies were scattered all over the place. They walked back to the rail track, dragging themselves toward the south.

As the days passed, they began to see numbers of Koreans, or Japanese, children as well as women, walking on the rails.

"Hey, are you Japanese or Koreans?" asked one elderly man in Japanese. He walked along with Hideyo and his group.

"We are Koreans. But not members of the Communist Party," Hideyo answered carefully in the Korean language. He was taking every possible precaution. There was a prize for producing anyone on the "wanted" list, dead or alive. Hideyo suspected that Korean Communists who had trained in

Manchuria were itching to get hold of his father. They would gladly slash the son's head. He would let no one know who he was, lest someone betray him to the Communists for a price. "Are you heading for the south?" he asked the old man in Korean.

"I am going back to Japan. If I can, that is. Too bad Japan has lost the war."

Hideyo almost screamed in his surprise. "Lost the war? Is the war over? When?" Shoichi, Shinzo, and Makoto all looked shocked, but they remained silent for they did not speak Korean as well as Hideyo.

"We've been working way up north," he told the man. "The Korean Communists attacked us and we've been walking ever since. I am heading for Seoul. What day is this?"

"The seventeenth of August." The man spoke in poor Korean. "It's all over. I heard the Emperor's talk over the radio." His voice cracked. "And I heard that the Americans dropped powerful bombs on Hiroshima and Nagasaki. It's over!" Tears streamed like a river on his deeply wrinkled face.

Hideyo wanted to comfort him, to tell him that he was a Japanese boy, his sadness was great too, but he held back and stayed cool. "When did the war end?" he asked.

"Two days ago. It's all over."

They heard more stories.

"No wonder everybody is heading southward," Shinzo whispered. "They're getting away from the Korean Communists. We've been walking fifteen days!"

They entered a railroad tunnel that became darker and darker. They stumbled on the ties. Hideyo and Makoto fumbled for the candles in their rucksacks and Makoto lit them. The candles gave a faint light, and carefully they went forward.

They felt vibration on the rails. A train! The boys stepped aside, but there was not much space between the rails and the wall of the tunnel. The engine passed by, roaring and shaking the tunnel, and the wind from the train blew out the candles.

Hideyo pasted himself against the wall and turned his head sideways. He could see sparks from the wheels, and they flew to his legs and hips and his skin burned. The thick, heavy smoke enveloped the tunnel, and he was unable to breathe or keep his eyes open. He coughed and coughed and felt dizzy. Is this the end of me? he thought. Still he clung to the wall. He heard a sound like something smashing and at the same time he felt warm water on his neck and face, running down to his chest.

At last the train passed. With deep relief, still coughing, Hideyo called his friends' names, and they answered. Again Makoto lit the candles and they went on carefully, touching the tunnel wall as a guide, for the candles did not give enough light.

Suddenly Hideyo stumbled and fell. Makoto, right behind him, fell too. Both candles went out.

"Hey, what's going on? Are you all right?" yelled Shinzo.

"I think I stumbled on a human," Hideyo replied. Once more Makoto lit the candles, and there lay the mangled body of the elderly Japanese, blocking the track.

They were glad when they saw a faint light in the far distance, and walked much faster, eager to swallow fresh air. They left the tunnel and took deep breaths. They were all splashed with blood from head to toe, and at first they thought they might be injured, but it was blood splashed from other escapees who could not get out of the way fast enough.

Looking for a thicket, they left the track and began

wiping off the blood with large leaves.

"Halt!" someone shouted in poor Korean. From an opposite thicket two Russian soldiers with machine guns came running.

The boys raised their arms high. If there were just one soldier, Hideyo thought, they could fight him, but there were two, with weapons.

"Are you Korean Communist members?" the Russian asked.

The boys answered as one. "We are!"

"Where are you going?"

"We are going to P'yŏnggang," Hideyo answered.

"Why are you carrying Japanese sacks and blankets?"

Hideyo lied. "We stole from the Japanese. Our parents got killed. We are heading for our relatives."

"Are you all brothers?" one of the soldiers asked.

"No, cousins. We are orphans." Hideyo made a sad face.

The soldiers stared at the boys and there was silence. Shoichi broke the stillness. "I have fine cigarettes. Do you want to smoke?"

"Where did you get them?" a soldier asked.

"I stole from the Japanese," answered Shoichi. "You've never tasted fine cigarettes like these." He reached to his chest pocket, his right arm still in the air. The soldiers came closer.

"Do you have food? Let's exchange," Shoichi said.

"No, we don't have food. Give me those cigarettes," commanded the head Russian.

Another, close to Shoichi, shouted, "You stink!"

"We have not bathed for almost two weeks," said Hideyo with a little laugh. And then Makoto and Shinzo began to laugh too.

With the laughter the soldiers seemed to relax. They let the boys bring their arms down. And as they puffed the fine Japanese cigarettes the taller soldier said that if they went on to the next town, Tanch'ŏn, they would find that the Communist Army Headquarters was hiring laborers for a little money. If they stayed on they would be fed.

Tanch'ŏn? Hideyo thought. They had only walked a fourth of the distance to Seoul. It's a long way to Seoul but I must make it. Hideyo talked to himself in his heart.

"Say, comrades." He spoke brightly to the Russian soldiers in Korean. He asked if there was a pond or river nearby, as he wanted to bathe before he met his relatives. The Russians said to walk a couple of miles to the west and he would cross a little river.

Once more the boys walked. They were thrilled to hear they would find a river but they did not run or show joyful faces. They walked slowly and composed themselves by singing Korean love songs loudly as they went.

The first thing they did when they came to the river was to fill their stomachs with water. They filled their canteens. Then they stripped, washed themselves, and rinsed the Korean clothes borrowed from the Lees. They spread the garments on the riverbank where the sun-heated rocks would dry them, and then they threw themselves on the warm rocks and went to sleep.

When they reached the army headquarters in Tanch'ŏn they learned that the labor was putting dead bodies into large straw sacks and tossing them from the cliff into Tanch'ŏn Bay. These were bodies that had been thrown from trains or left to die in the fields. At the end of the day they were given cooked cabbage and rice. Each time, the four boys saved a little, for they knew they had many miles ahead of them.

Whenever the boys handled a dead woman or a young girl they took extra care, sliding the sacks gently down the cliff into the water. Hideyo was very relieved that he did not see his mother's or his sisters' bodies.

When the work was finished, headquarters gave them their small earnings. Then they walked on. They walked for a month and a half until they reached the port city, Wŏnsan. It was the end of September now, and the companions decided to part. Makoto would go with Shinzo and Shoichi to their relatives, Hideyo would go on to Seoul. He was determined to get at least as far as the thirty-eighth parallel, beyond which lay some safety and the hope of meeting his mother and sisters later in Seoul. They cooked the last of their rice and shared the water from the canteens. They lay in the mountain bush, reminiscing about their wonderful friendship.

"Hey," Makoto said, "if we ever get back to Japan, where shall we meet?"

"At Tokyo Bridge. It's a famous meeting spot," Shoichi suggested.

"When?" asked Shinzo.

"Maybe five years from now," answered Hideyo.

The stars shone brightly above them, but the breeze from the bay held the smell of fall. None of the four young men could sleep for thinking of this, their last night together. As night advanced Hideyo began to feel chilly, and he spread his little sister's tiny fur coat on his back and covered himself with his blanket.

Hideyo alone headed toward Seoul next morning. He felt lonesome, with no one to talk to, but he kept walking on the railroad tracks, holding the dream that soon he would meet with his mother and sisters.

Chapter 5

Ko, tall and broad-shouldered, was well suited to the army uniform and looked like a real soldier. Mother was short and slightly built and looked awkward in the high-necked khaki outfit. Her dusty hair was covered by a soldier's hat.

Even though Ko rolled my trousers, they kept unrolling and dragged on the ground.

I could not see my hands, only long sleeves flip-flopping.

The baggy trousers kept falling down even when tied with the rope Mother had tied my wrist with. Ko made rope suspenders for me.

But soon the edge of the trousers rubbed against my chest. My right ear was throbbing. It still felt plugged and I could not hear when Mother or Ko talked to me from the right side.

Mother comforted me. "Give it a chance." But the August sun was hot on my shaved head, my mouth was dry, and my entire body ached. I whined.

"Gosh! Whiny sister! Can't you shut up for a change?" Ko was disgusted.

"I hurt!"

She gave me a harsh look. "Just shut up and keep on walking."

I cried as I walked, wiping my eyes and nose with my uniform sleeves. "Save your body water," Ko told me. "With each tear you are dehydrating yourself."

I shaded my head with one hand and shed more tears over my shaved head. "It will grow back," Ko said without emotion.

I pitied myself for not hearing well and for the

constant pain in my chest. And I was mad at Ko. "Shut up!" she was always saying, or "Walk!" and Mother never corrected her for her rough talk. I longed for Father. If Father were here, Ko would still be spunky but a tender sister. Finally my crying got on Mother's nerves.

"Why can't you be strong and good like your honorable sister?" she asked, wiping her forehead.

I yelled. "I'm not her! She'd cry too if she'd got hit."

"I would not!" Ko snapped. "You have done nothing but whine and fuss. This journey would be easier if you had got killed!"

I stopped walking and stared at her, dumbfounded. My big sister wished me dead.

"Ko, don't you ever talk like that again!" Mother said. "Do you understand? Never!"

Ko just walked faster. Faster and faster. Mother took my hand and we followed at a slower pace.

The tracks were entering mountains. The shade of the tall trees was cool, and I picked leaves and sucked their juice, but it was bitter.

Ko was out of sight, but suddenly her voice came from a thicket. When she appeared, she was smiling at us. "Do you want to rest, Little One?"

I was not going to speak to a sister who wished me dead.

"Let's rest, Mother," Ko repeated.

Deep inside, I hoped we were going to rest. I was dry and starved, but mostly I longed to lie down. The pain in my ear and in my chest seemed unbearable. Mother and I kept on walking. "Aren't you ever hungry?" I asked Mother, because she never complained.

"I am very hungry and tired, but what good would it do to complain?" she said. "I am grateful we are

alive. We must make it to Seoul and meet Hideyo."
She choked with tears.

Ko called again, this time from the top of a hill,
and waved to us to come up. We puffed our way up
and she led us to a small cave. I knew she wanted to
make up for what she had said, but I sulked. I
dropped my rucksack, took off the heavy, smelly
uniform, threw myself on the ground, and fell asleep.

Then Ko was shaking me gently. "Little One. It's
dinner time." Something smelled good and I sat up.
Mother was eating corn on the cob. Ko was eating a
red, juicy tomato. She took an ear of corn from the
campfire, rolled it in a cloth, and handed it to me. I
gazed at the food with my mouth open.

"Eat it before it gets cold," Ko said. "It's
delicious."

I had forgotten that I was angry at her. "Where did
you get it, Honorable Sister?"

"I'll tell you when you've eaten."

Hungry as I was, I had a hard time eating.
Swallowing was difficult and my chest felt tight. I
took small bites.

Ko told her story. She had looked for a stream and
found a cornfield. All she thought of was bringing an
armful of corn to surprise Mother and me. Then the
Korean farmer caught her. He called her a damned
Japanese and told her to drop the corn.

Ko, in her perfect Korean, had denied she was
Japanese. She had told him her little sister was
wounded, that her mother was with her. "The
Japanese army police chased us away from Nanam,"
she told him, "and we are heading for relatives in
Seoul. We are starving."

He asked whether she was a boy or a girl and she
told him about Mother shaving her head.

The man hated the Japanese. He had been lying in

wait for thieves who stole his vegetables. It would be a great day, he said, when they lost the war, and he spat on the ground.

Then he let Ko fill the canteens at his well, picked ripe tomatoes for her, and gave her a burlap sack to fill with corn.

Mother gave a deep sigh when Ko's story was finished. She had never expected Ko to become a liar and robber. "I had to," Ko said.

She roasted all the ears of corn, to take with us. For the first time since we had left home I went to sleep without fear of attack and with a full stomach.

Ko rearranged our rucksacks at dawn. Now I was to carry the light things—aluminum mess kits, knives, matches, candles. Mother had the corn. Ko carried the heaviest bundle. I had to put on the heavy uniform again. We walked.

One morning slopes began to flatten and we saw people coming across the fields. My chest began hurting again and my earache persisted, but I did not cry anymore for I did not want Ko to wish I was dead.

Now we saw men carrying rucksacks and bundles and women carrying babies on their backs with a wide sash, Japanese-style.

Mother called, "Excuse me." They stopped and looked us over. "Are you going to Seoul?" Mother asked in elegant Japanese. They still stared at us. "We are Japanese," said Mother.

"You're wearing Korean Communist Army clothes," a man said.

"Excuse our appearance." Mother bowed slightly. "We had to disguise ourselves."

"Where are you from?"

"Far north. Nanam."

"That's almost in Manchuria!" the man said.

"You've been walking all this time?"

Mother explained about the train. Then the man told us that he had sold his barbershop in a nearby town to a Korean friend. He was returning to Japan with his relatives. "Since Koreans began attacking Japanese, we cannot sleep peacefully."

Mother asked where we were. The man pointed. "The brown roof you see in the distance is the Seoul station."

At last! I could not believe it. A bath house, Mother had said, a good place to sleep and maybe plenty to eat!

Without warning we found ourselves at the end of a seemingly endless line of people. "What is this?" Ko asked the last man in line. He wore Korean clothes so she spoke Korean.

"This is the checkpoint for escapees. We must show what we bring."

These people had little to show, and we were almost there when two armed Japanese policemen, a stout one and a tall one, suddenly shouted and pointed their guns at us. I trembled and my ear and chest began throbbing.

They questioned us. We were wearing Korean Communist Army uniforms—were we seeking political asylum? Ko told them we were Japanese. Where were we from? Could we prove this?

Mother showed our insurance documents and school report cards. Finally the men put their guns down. We had reached the head of the line now.

The interrogation went on. Did we carry a large amount of money? A little cash, Mother said, bringing a pouch from her shirt pocket. They checked and gave it back. Did we have a savings book?

"Yes," Mother said and looked through her bundle. She pulled out everything but there was no savings book. "I must have left it," Mother said in tears of distress.

"We will have to search you," they said.

They went through our clothes, all our pockets, and the rucksacks, but no savings book was found.

They found the roasted corn. What was this? Our food supply, Ko told them.

Finally the stout policeman asked where we were going, and Mother told him we would stay in Seoul until her son arrived. When the war was over we would return to Nanam.

"The war is over," he said.

We were stupefied. "When?" Ko asked.

"Yesterday. You cannot go back. That is why there are so many escapees from the north. The Japanese are in peril in Korea now."

"What is today?" Ko asked.

August sixteenth. Hadn't we heard about the atomic bombs dropped on Nagasaki and Hiroshima? No.

"Japan lost," the tall policeman told us. "Those two cities have turned to hell."

Suddenly Mother dropped to the ground.

Ko loosened Mother's collar and, as usual, I cried. Some men standing about were told to carry Mother into the station. The stout policeman ran for a bottle, and I smelled whiskey. They poured some into Mother's mouth, and Ko unbuttoned the uniform front and massaged her chest and arms. I was overjoyed when she opened her eyes.

"I must have blacked out." She tried to get up, but the police told her to stay where she was. They were friendlier now, but the interrogation continued. We were told we must be sprayed with chemicals to kill lice and bugs we might have carried from the north. We must take off our clothes.

Mother got up and took off all but the thin chemise she wore under her shirt. They sprayed her from head to toe, also the uniform she had worn. I was relieved that they did not notice the short sword against her skin. Then Mother put on her own clothes. How much more comfortable she looked.

Ko was next, then my turn came. The men said something and laughed and I stood, hesitant about removing my uniform. "They say they never saw such a tiny soldier!" said one. "Now take off your uniform."

My chemise was stained with blood. The men were shocked. "You were wounded," the stout policeman said. "How?" Ko told him.

I was sprayed and the powder stung. I screamed. Then Mother handed me my own clothes. They were not clean but, oh, how much more comfortable I felt in them. I hoped I would never have to wear that uniform again. But Ko and Mother were folding the uniforms neatly and putting them into the clothes bundle.

"We have no winter clothes," Mother explained.

They told us we could go, and we were leaving when the stout policeman stopped us. "Have your little daughter's wound treated," he said.

We followed his directions to a group of large tents with red crosses painted on their roofs. Was this the Japanese hospital? Ko asked a medic who sat at a desk outside.

"Right," he told her. He saw my blouse stained with blood. "Come," he said. He took my sack, and Mother and Ko followed to a cot where he told me to lie down. He took off my blouse.

A young doctor came. "I am Doctor Takeda," he said. Mother and Ko bowed. He pulled up a small stool and asked my name.

"Kawashima Yoko."

"How old?"

"Almost twelve."

He was filling in a form. "Tell me what happened."

I told him, and about my ear aching and being deaf. He asked how long ago and I told him six days.

When he pulled my chemise carefully from the wound and examined my injury, he shook his head. "I don't see how she could have stood it all this time. It is badly infected."

"My little sister did very well," Ko told him.

He sterilized the place beneath my right breast that was burned and infected, applied medicine, and the medic put on antiseptic gauze and wrapped my chest. "Now let me see your ear." The doctor put a round mirror with a hole in the center on his head.

He pulled my earlobe down and inserted a long thin wire. Tears streaming, I gritted my teeth and saw Mother's agonized face. He showed me a piece of metal. "This was in your ear. Your eardrum has been punctured and it is infected." He drained the infection, dropped in some medicine, and stuffed cotton in my ear.

As he added information to his form he asked, "By chance, is your father's name Yoshio?"

"Yes," Mother said.

"I know him," said the doctor. "My father and your husband were classmates at the University. My father is Kazuzo Takeda—he's a member of the House of Peers. They get together at our house every year after their alumni association meeting."

"I know him!" Mother cried.

Doctor Takeda told her that he had been assigned to the Japanese Army Hospital here six months ago, before the war ended. He asked Mother her plans and she told him about waiting for Hideyo.

"Your little daughter should stay in the hospital," he told her. "She is badly infected and needs treatment every day."

I was given a mat in the crowded patients' tent and Mother stayed with me that night while Ko took her blanket, canteen, and two ears of corn back to the station. Mother fell asleep guarding what little we possessed, but, throbbing and burning and disturbed by the cries of other patients, I could not sleep. In the night the medic brought me powdered medicine in transparent paper and at last I drifted off.

The sun was bright when I woke, and Mother was combing her hair. It was more gray than black now, and her face, once so beautiful, was deeply lined. She smiled at me, tying her hair at the back. "Wake up now, Little One. The doctor was here but he let you sleep. He wants to change your dressing." She handed me a damp cloth and I wiped my face. "Here is the canteen. Wash your mouth outside and go see the doctor."

My ear felt no better and I could not hold my head upright. The doctor took out the cotton, wet with pus, cleaned with the swab, and dropped in more medicine. Again I shed tears with the pain. He told me the swelling would go away and that I must have complete rest. Then the medic bandaged my chest.

I was leaving when the doctor stopped me and handed me a bottle of milk. "Each patient has a bottle a day," he told me.

I stared at the creamy milk. Holding the precious treasure in both hands, I stood still. Then I gathered my courage. "May I beg two more bottles?"

"For your honorable mother and sister?" the doctor asked. I nodded. He nodded too, and the medic gave me two more. I bowed to them deeply and walked as fast as I could to where Mother waited.

I stayed in the hospital tent two weeks, Mother and Ko taking turns being with me. As I watched Mother walking now I saw that her walk was feeble. She seemed smaller and smaller.

Either Mother or Ko was always at the station, waiting for Hideyo's arrival. But there was no Hideyo.

On September first the doctor spoke with Mother. "All patients will leave for Pusan by truck by the end of the month. A hospital ship will be leaving from there for Japan on October second. Come with us back to our homeland."

But Mother would wait for Hideyo. So on the last day of my hospital stay, Doctor Takeda gave us three bottles of milk, extra bandages, medicines, and cotton. He said I had made a good recovery but must take things easy and not catch a cold. He gave me a bottle of aspirin. "One tablet every three hours when the pain comes." He and Mother promised to meet in the homeland, fate willing.

We carried all of our belongings back to the station. The station was crowded with escapees from the north who had not found homes, Japanese soldiers released from the army, and civilians, all wanting to take the train to Pusan.

We sat outside and whenever a train, passenger or freight, pulled in, Mother and Ko would dash to the platform. I was to save our spot and guard our belongings. No Hideyo.

We drank some milk.

There was no food when night came. Then Ko said there would be no train until early morning and we must sleep. We found a small space on a bench in the waiting room and Ko squeezed Mother into it. She pushed our clothes bundle under the bench and she and I catnapped at Mother's feet.

As the night advanced I was so cold that I shivered, and my ear and chest ached. I crawled out. "I'm cold!" I said to Mother.

She took me on her lap and wrapped us both in her blanket. Secure in her arms, I went to sleep. But some time later there was a violent altercation with the man next to Mother, who complained that I had kicked him. I hadn't meant to. But Mother told Ko to give her the clothes bundle, and she pulled out my red overcoat and got it on me. She got out the Communist Army uniform and ordered me to put it on over the overcoat. Then she sent me back to my bed under the bench, where I cuddled up to Ko for warmth.

Mother was on the platform when the early train pulled in. Our neighbor tried to take her place while she was gone, but Ko said she would kill him with her peeling knife and he backed off. Mother came back without Hideyo and we drank the last of our milk.

"I will go and find food," Ko said, and took her empty rucksack. Another train came in and Mother rushed to the platform.

Then an elderly Japanese crawled under the bench and tried to take our clothes bundle. He claimed it was his. It was only when Mother returned and shouted, "Help! Thief!" that he gave up.

Ko came back with her rucksack partly filled with food from the hotel garbage. Mother was almost speechless at the cunning Ko had developed and her technique of swimming through danger.

While we lived at the station, the American soldiers came to Seoul. Confined to our small area, we hardly ever saw them.

One day when Ko returned she brought out from the rucksack some orange and apple peelings and several slices of bread. She had taken them from garbage cans at the former Japanese hospital now used by the American medical team.

We needed to bathe. We dared not leave our belongings at the station so we carried everything to the river. Autumn had come now, but still many people were bathing. Ko and Mother went into the water in chemise and panties while I stayed with the belongings. I saw Ko duck her head in the water, and Mother soaped it and began to shave. The sword's short blade sparkled again and again.

Then it was my turn. The water was very cold and Mother's fingers, soaping my back and my head, careful to avoid my chest and not get water in my ear, were icy. Even colder was the sharp blade that slid over my head. Mother changed my dressing and put drops in my ear. She said the new skin was growing nicely. I put on dry underwear and Ko rinsed all our wet underclothes and spread them on the rocks to dry.

We had been in Seoul for five weeks when one day Ko brought a warning. "We must get out of Seoul. I saw several Korean men dragging girls to the thicket and I saw one man raping a young girl." Ko was shivering. "The girls were screaming for help in Japanese. Will you shave my hair again now?"

At the river Mother shaved both our heads. Then she bound Ko's breasts tightly with the long cloth Dr. Takeda had used to wrap my chest, so that she would look even more like a boy. We all put on our filthy uniforms, protection against the chilly autumn air.

Back at the station our spots were taken so we sat outside in the warmth of the sun.

Mother interviewed the stationmaster. She told him we could not afford to ride to Pusan as passengers and would have to go on a freight car. He told her so many were heading for the port that he doubted we could even get on. The trip took two and a half days.

"Let us take last freight train tomorrow," Mother decided. "Perhaps Hideyo will be on it when it comes."

Ko and I carved word to Hideyo on the station posts and wherever we found wood. "Hideyo. To Pusan," I carved, hoping desperately that he would come before we left.

Then Ko took me to the narrow alley of the hospital and told me to hunt for food in the garbage cans. I opened a can and the strong rotten smell went through my nose. I could not put my hand into that garbage.

"Do it!" Ko ordered sharply. She was poking through a can with her jackknife. Already her sack was half filled.

I gagged. "I cannot, Honorable Sister."

"Go find sticks," Ko said.

Finally, with chopsticks I found, she showed me how to look for food. I found a half-eaten jelly sandwich, a meat sandwich, and lots of potato strips fried in oil, some cheese, and lettuce. These were our food supplies for the train trip. We rushed back to where Mother guarded our belongings, ate, and sat through the night.

It was three o'clock the next afternoon when the last freight train pulled in. In vain we looked for Hideyo. Everyone—Japanese, Koreans, young, old, children, feeble people—were trying to get on the train. Mother held my hand tightly and Ko, ahead of us, made her way, bumping people with her large bundle.

The first boxcar was packed. "No room!" a man shouted.

The next one was even worse and still many were trying to crawl in. Others were clinging to the edge of the train.

"Try the flatcar!" Ko yelled. The train whistled.

The flatcar was piled with lumber and people, but a Japanese man on the train called to us. "Come here! Quick!" Ko handed him her bundle. Knowing my chest was tender, she lifted me like a baby and handed me to the man, who dropped me on some lumber and extended his arms to Mother. She was on. Ko tossed up our rucksacks.

The train whistled three times and began moving. "Honorable Sister, hurry!" I screamed.

She jumped, the man pulled, and he and Mother pulled Ko onto the car.

"Oh!" Mother bowed deeply to the man. "Thank you!"

"A close call," he replied. I saw him now for the first time, elderly with a white beard, with a gentle way of speaking.

We swayed on the flatcar, and the wind blew so hard that when Ko opened my rucksack the wind almost blew our food away. She handed our elderly friend a cheese sandwich. "I have not eaten for three days," he told her, and devoured it.

Night came and I shivered with cold. Ko and Mother got out coats and uniforms, clutching them tightly lest the wind take them away. Wrapped in my blanket too, I clung to Ko.

In the morning we ate whatever was not spoiled of the fruit, sharing with the old gentleman. Ko gave him bread and he was overjoyed. "This is moldy but better than none," he said.

At one point the train stopped and we watched a man jump off, turn his back, and urinate. Then he called to us. "If you have to go, go now. No telling when we'll stop again." We managed to get off and squat right there, shielding each other.

On the train jolted, south to Pusan. Now I felt not only cold but feverish. My throat was sore and I had lost my voice. But I did not whine because these were nothing compared with the pain I had been through with ear and chest. And at last, on the third day, the train pulled into the Pusan station.

The station was packed. We must go to the warehouse by the harbor. "I must wait here for my son," Mother told a Korean official.

"You cannot. We are going to have our Independence celebration here. Go!"

I did not think I could walk an inch farther, for I was burning with fever now and my head pounded. But we dragged on. Koreans of all ages, dressed in their best and carrying flags, were heading for the celebration at the station, and there were American soldiers too, with cameras.

The warehouse had belonged to the Japanese navy until the war ended, and slogans were still large on the walls. "Victory!" "Attack with Courage!" "Great Imperial Navy!" Now the warehouse was filled with people.

Again it was Ko who found a corner, and I put my blanket on the concrete floor and fell asleep. But I was not allowed to sleep long. A man was yelling at me, telling me to sit up and make room for him. Mother told him I was ill but he looked about to choke her. At that, I grabbed his legs and he fell. Angrier than ever, he got up and came toward me, threatening.

Then I saw Mother, the sword blade pointing at his chest. "Try and touch her!" she said in a low voice. And the man went away.

"Lie down, Little One," Mother said as if nothing

had happened. "Save your sister's spot." She put the blade into its sheath.

Ko brought orange peels and rotten apples she had found near a mess hall. There were peaches too and plenty of those fried potato strips.

"I have to go to the toilet," I said.

There were six toilets at the end of the building for us to squat on, but no doors and no separate toilets for men and women. A woman ahead of us, embarrassed, pulled down her trousers and panty and squatted, and I tried not to look at her. Then Mother went and stood in front of her, and I saw the young woman come out. In a moment she screamed for help. I turned to see that she had been seized by four men at the end of our line. There was nothing we could do.

When we got back to our space Ko wanted to go. Mother's lips were pale. "Is the wrapper around your breasts tight?" she asked. "Ko, you must do it the way boys do."

From then on we did it the way boys do. It was awful. We were wet and our clothes were wet. But we were safer.

That day was a nightmare. Drunken Koreans, celebrating their independence, were all around us. One who swayed back and forth demanded of Ko, "Are you a boy or a girl?"

"A boy," she answered.

"You sound like a girl. Let me feel."

"Go ahead," Ko said.

How I prayed someone would come to rescue us. No one was trying to help young women, for they knew that if they made the Koreans even angrier they might burn down this warehouse and the people in it. The Koreans were free of the Japanese Empire after all those years. The drunken man put his large hand on Ko's chest. "Flat," he said. "Boys are no fun."

The group of men left us but they staggered among the people, hunting maidens for their pleasure, and whenever they found one they dragged her outside. Women's shrieks echoed.

Mother and Ko did not sleep that night. In the morning their eyes were bloodshot and they looked worn out. Ko said she must sleep and I must go for food. She gave me directions.

Voice still missing, head pounding, throat aching, ear throbbing, I put my rucksack on my head as the Koreans did and headed for the building Ko had directed me to. With a maple branch broken from a tree I poked through garbage cans. There were milk cartons with a few drops in them. Flour in bags. We could make a fire outside and mix flour and water for dumplings. There was bread half-eaten. Browned bananas—what a treasure. I ate a banana as I poked through. Soon I put my filled sack on my head and started back.

At a small stream I stopped to drink and I heard a cry. In the weeds was a Korean man on top of a girl. She was kicking wildly and screaming. My knees began to shake, and, holding my sack on my head with both hands, I walked as fast as I could to Ko and Mother.

"We cannot stay here any longer," Mother said when I told her. "We must get to Japan." Her eyes filled. "But Hideyo. He will be all alone in Korea."

A week later it was announced that a cargo ship was coming and could take a hundred people to Japan. Japanese must surrender any dangerous weapons— guns, knives. We must get in line for the ship.

With all the others we scrambled for the line. "I cannot surrender our precious sword," Mother whispered.

"You must not," Ko agreed. "Let us go to the toilet. Stay in line and guard our belongings, Little One."

When they came back Ko was walking strangely, her left leg not bending. "Little One," said Mother in a low voice, "your sister's leg is wounded. She has a cast on it. You understand." I nodded.

When the ship finally docked the Korean official counted one hundred. "Ninety-seven, ninety-eight, ninety-nine, and one hundred!"

There was a cry. "Please, officer!" It was a middle-aged Japanese woman. "Please let my father come with me!"

"No. The rule is the rule." This official, like all Korean officials, looked harsh to me. "That is what your government always said to us."

"He is old and he needs my care. I will pay! Please."

"The rule is the rule."

Then a man behind the old father offered to change places, so both the woman and her father stayed behind.

I watched the boat fade away toward the horizon and wondered how long I would have to wait until I was on a ship to the homeland I had dreamed of all of my life.

A hundred had left but more hundreds poured in, and we continued to wait in line, not daring to leave lest we miss our chance on the next boat. A week later the ship returned, but we were not among this hundred.

Mother continued to search among the crowds for Hideyo. Ko, walking awkwardly, her left leg stiff, went searching for food.

Rain came. We covered ourselves with our blankets but soon we were soaked. It rained for three days and we sat on the ground, in line, day and night. Our belongings were sodden.

I began to cough and Ko remembered the aspirin Doctor Takeda had given us. Somehow it had slipped our minds until now. We all took aspirin, crushing the sour tablets with our teeth.

At last we saw the ship again, and when Ko went to the toilet she counted the people. We were seventy-nine, eighty, and eighty-one.

They began loading early in the morning. As each one walked onto the gangplank, Korean officials inspected belongings. They touched our bodies to make sure we were not carrying concealed weapons.

They searched me first and I winced with pain when my chest was touched. Then I began to cough and could not stop. I pulled up my uniform jacket to show where I was bandaged. "Go," the official said.

I was afraid for Ko, carrying our family treasure. The official checked her sack and found nothing but food from the garbage. He touched her chest, sides, back, and hips. His hands moved toward her thigh. Ko's face was white and I trembled. The official must feel the gauze that tied the sword. He was feeling the gauze.

"My leg is wounded. Don't press hard, you are hurting me." Ko grimaced as if in pain.

"Go," said the man. I made myself stay calm.

They let Mother through easily with the filthy, damp clothes in her bundle, but they took the small nail scissors.

There was space on the ship and we spread a blanket and sat on it. Ko handed me a slice of moldy bread and I wiped off the mold on my trousers and ate it. When the sun tinted the sea a brilliant red the boat slowly left the dock.

"At last! No more fear," said Ko. She leaned against the rail.

At last. Soon I would be meeting my grandmother and seeing my beautiful homeland. I joined Ko at the rail. Mother sat still on the blanket, head buried in her arms. Her hair, all gray now, blew in the wind.

Ko kept staring at the Korean peninsula, fading away slowly, and tears were falling on her cheek. It was the first time I had seen Ko cry since we left home. Quietly I went to sit close to Mother, whose face also was wet with tears that she could not stop.

Chapter 6

The tracks separated, heading in two directions. Hideyo stood there. Which way? He looked at the sun, which was going down, and using the sun as his guide, he took the southwest track to Seoul.

As dark was coming on, the tracks entered a narrow gorge through mountains, and Hideyo decided that he might be able to find mushrooms. He had eaten almost nothing since he had left his friends two weeks before.

He was not only hungry but terribly lonely. To ease his loneliness he had thought about Shoichi, Shinzo, and Makoto and all the doings he had shared with them since kindergarten days. He had even smiled, remembering some of their mischief.

He got off the track to hunt for mushrooms and decided to camp there, for there was no moon and he could not see to go on. Mushrooms were plentiful. He stuffed them in the pockets of his trousers and shirt and the side pockets of his rucksack. Then he built a small fire. Roasting and eating mushrooms, he thought of his mother and sisters and wondered how they were faring—if they were still alive. He thought of the bankbook he was carrying and wondered if his mother had any money.

He looked up at the twilight sky at the sound of geese, flying in V formation, heading toward somewhere warm. All talked excitedly as they flew, and Hideyo wished he were one of them. I must hurry, he told himself, I must get to Seoul.

He let the fire die. He would sleep until dawn. Going deeper into the forest, he spread his little sister's fur coat beneath him and curled up in his blanket. The ground was damp and the wind bit sharply through his summer clothes.

Suddenly he awoke. In complete darkness he sat up and listened. There were human voices mingling with the wind and coming toward him. Speaking Korean. Hideyo pushed his blanket and rucksack into the trees and covered his head with the fur coat, hoping he looked like an animal.

"The campfire was still warm," a voice said. "The escapee cannot have gone too far in the dark." The footsteps came nearer and nearer, and a powerful flashlight blinded Hideyo. Korean Communist Army, he thought, patrolling the mountain. How many? Silently he pulled his jackknife from his pocket.

The searching footsteps went this way and that. Hideyo's heartbeats went faster and louder.

"Not much use looking in the dark," said the same voice.

"Let's go back to the squadron and patrol early in the morning," said another voice. "Anyhow, we've caught more than enough today."

"How many?" a different voice asked.

"Sixteen. Seven Japs, the others Communist resisters."

The flashlight was still circling and several times aimed at the tree where Hideyo was hiding. It came closer. Hideyo shrank behind the tree, still holding his jackknife in his right hand, prepared.

"I don't see anybody. Let's go."

The voices and the flashlight were moving away, but the wind carried the voices clearly to where Hideyo hid. Finally they died away. Again he covered himself with his blanket. He was exhausted but he could not fall asleep right away for fear he would not wake early, before the patrol came back. If I had that flashlight, he thought, I'd cover the light and walk.

He did wake when the forest was dark but pale pink showed in the eastern sky. Quickly he rolled the little fur coat in the blanket, draped it over the rucksack on his shoulders, and headed down to the tracks. That was the shortest way to Seoul.

The mountain became lighter and lighter as the sun rose. He had gone deep into the forest the night before and now he was not sure of his direction. Again he used the sun as his guide. He came to a clearing that dropped off in a sharp cliff, and, holding branches of trees, he went down the cliff. Lo, there were the shiny tracks stretching for miles toward Seoul. He stopped and took a deep breath of relief.

Then, on the tracks some distance ahead of him, he saw people walking.

Maybe they are all escapees, he thought, excited. He was very happy to see them after his great loneliness. He ran down the rest of the cliff and took fast steps to catch up.

Suddenly machine gun shots burst in the air beyond where the people were walking. Hideyo froze. Then he ran back up the cliff and headed in the direction of the shots. They trapped those people! Damn, damn, damn! He spoke to himself.

The clearing became woods. No path, but he pushed through.

There was commotion on the tracks below. He seemed to be above the spot where the people had been shot, but he did not dare go down the cliff to look.

"All dead." The voice speaking Korean came up to him.

"Check their belongings. Take all valuables," said another voice. "Strip the bodies. If they have gold fillings, pull out their teeth."

Hideyo was shaking. He waited.

"All stripped," a voice shouted.

The soldiers were climbing the cliff, and he looked frantically around for a hiding place. There was no thicket, and they would see him if he ran for shelter. Except for one tall pine, the trees were not large enough to hide him. Shall I play dead? he thought. Then they would strip him, pull out his gold-filled tooth, and take the savings book.

The men were much closer. Still carrying his rucksack, draping the blanket over his shoulders, Hideyo climbed the pine tree. As he climbed, the blanket slipped, the fur coat appeared, and his Korean pants caught on the sharp branch and tore. If I drop this coat it will be the end, he thought. Clutching the tree with his left arm, he yanked the fur coat from the blanket, gripped the sleeve in his teeth, and climbed until he reached a thick branch. Hugging coat and blanket, he sat.

Yes, they were Korean Communist soldiers, four of them, and they had climbed the cliff with bags full of plunder. They must hide here, watching for escapees on the tracks, Hideyo thought.

"Let's divide what we got." Hideyo recognized a voice from the night before.

"Not now. Meet me at my house and we'll divide there." A short soldier seemed to be head of the group.

"You'll take all you want and give us junk again," the deep voice said.

"Yeah!" another agreed.

"Shut up and do as I say."

"No. Divide the treasures now or I will report you!"

Suddenly the short soldier's machine gun went off, the loud burst echoing on the mountain. Smoke rose to where Hideyo was sitting.

"Now, you want to be dead or do as I say?" said the head of the group, and he looked down coolly at the man he had just killed, and walked off.

The others stood there. They looked at each other. The wind blew, the pine tree swayed, and Hideyo prayed the branch where he sat would not break. He held tightly to the blanket and the coat and tried not to put too much weight on the branch.

The killer was stalking toward the east, his gun on his shoulders. The other two, still staring at the dead man, finally picked up the leader's large bag and ran to catch up.

Hideyo stayed on the branch until everything was quiet. He dropped the blanket and coat, then slid down carefully. He checked the dead soldier's gun, but the bullets were gone so there was no use taking it. Also, it would be heavy to carry. Quickly he headed southwest.

But he stopped and went back. Carefully he removed the uniform from the still-warm body. The clothes would be useful, as the Korean outfit he was wearing was badly torn. The jacket was soaked with blood but Hideyo crammed it into his rucksack. He untied the dead man's shoes and tried one on. Too small.

He walked all day, keeping to the woods even though there was no path. Below, a glimpse of the tracks now and then was his guide. The moon came up and he dragged on. Now it was getting cold, and he pulled all his underwear, socks, and his student's uniform from the rucksack and put them on. On top of those he wore the thin, badly worn Korean clothes borrowed from the Lees. Somehow he could not throw away these garments, perhaps because he had loved the Lees.

He began to lose track of dates and months. All he

knew was that fall was there because the trees turned to bright colors and some already stood naked and shivering when the wind blew. He had found no water since he had strayed to the mountain. On top of that, a diet of mushrooms had caused severe diarrhea and his stomach ached.

Finally he had to rest. As soon as he found a suitable place, maybe a small burrow, he would sleep. He was terribly cold. The moon shone over the entire earth to give light, but why did it not give heat to warm him? He thought the beautiful moon was most unsympathetic. He found a spot and went to sleep.

When he awoke in the morning heavy frost surrounded him. He took deep breaths and saw them in the air as steam. His feet were numb. Hunger pains struck him and he sensed that he would soon starve.

He'd freeze to death if he did not keep on walking.

He covered his head with the tiny fur coat, got the rucksack on his back, and caped himself with the blanket. He started to walk but he was so weary he could not walk fast.

Between the trees he saw a vegetable field. Food! He dragged himself down to the field but nothing was left there but frozen clods of earth. He pushed himself back to the mountain thicket, and went on.

There were times when he wanted to give up walking and fall asleep on the frosty ground, but something told him that if he did he would never wake up in this world.

It began to snow. In Nanam he had been delighted to see snow come, but now he hated it. He looked up at the sky and opened his mouth wide, trying to catch some flakes, but the snow did not fill his hungry stomach.

I must live through this, he thought. I want to see Mother and my sisters. They must be having a bad time too. I've got to make it to Seoul! He talked to himself. The thought of Father, so lost and far away, came too.

The snow turned into a blizzard. His shoes, rubber-soled tabi, were torn to shreds, his Korean clothes were frozen, and he was totally exhausted. He could not see an inch ahead. He sat down by the roots of a large tree and rested. So drowsy. He shook his head to wake himself. I cannot die here, he thought. But how long can I walk without food?

The tears streamed and stung his chapped face. His hands, cracked open, bled. His eyelashes were freezing and he blinked many times.

He decided that he would try to walk once more. Using all his energy, he stood up. He took one step, slipped, and fell. He had no strength to brace himself against the blizzard. Again he got up, took a step. Whenever he fell he had a hard time getting up, and the rucksack felt like tons of stone on his back.

Suddenly in the distance, between the trees, in the blizzard, he saw a faint red light. He stopped and looked. Now nothing. Then the light again. Was it his imagination playing a trick on him? Or could it be a farmhouse? He focused his eyes on the light; then it disappeared. He took off his glasses, trying to wipe them, but his clothes were frozen. Whatever it is, I must walk there. I must! This time he saw the light clearly. He took one step, another, and another. He got caught by branches, stumbled over the tree roots, and fell. He lay there, no energy left.

Then he lifted his head and began to crawl toward the light. It looked warm. He found that he was crawling down a mountain slope. Twigs slapped his face, his entire body felt numb. Now he was lying on the ground. I've got to get there! Again he focused on the light. It was still there, as if to tell Hideyo to hurry and come.

He got to his feet. He felt terribly dizzy and staggered, but he dragged on. To the light, to the light. At last he reached a small farmhouse, lost all control, and collapsed.

Chapter 7

"That is our homeland, Little One." Mother pointed from the ship to where the island floated in the deep morning fog. Miles of soft hills linked together.

We had been three days crossing the rough Korean Strait, and at last we were entering the Japanese zone of Tsushima Strait. In spite of seasickness I was excited. We would be landing in our own country, welcomed and safe. Our grandparents would feed us and give us fine beds. I leaned on the guardrail and watched the island come closer and closer. I was already carrying my rucksack and wearing my blanket.

When the ship docked at Fukuoka, a Japanese man wearing a white arm band that said "Committee" stood at the foot of the gangplank. Using a megaphone, he was saying something over and over, but I could not understand his southern accent. Mother said he was telling the refugees to find their places. We looked for a large "K," and soon forty of us stood beneath the sign. A man at a desk, his face blank, took our names and a young committee member told the "K" group to follow him to the refugee camp.

All these years I had dreamed of my beautiful homeland and its cheerful people, and now I was completely taken aback by demolished Fukuoka. Burned fields, wrecked houses and buildings. What trees there were stood painfully without branches and with deep scars of fire. The sky was clear and crisp but I saw not a bird. Isn't there one bird to sing and welcome us? I thought, searching the sky. Besides, the attitude of the men we had seen seemed to say, "Why did you come? We could do without you."

"Watch out!" Ko told me. I tripped on the cracked asphalt road and fell.

I got up, and I saw that my left shoe had split open at the toe and had separated from the sole. I had to lift that leg much higher, the sole flapping. The fall wind began to bite me and my shaven head.

We walked for two hours. The refugee camp was the auditorium of a girls' school, and the hundred who got off the ship were to stay there until we found someplace to go. It was small, and again we were squashed against each other. Mother, Ko, and I found a corner, dropped our burdens on the floor, and rested.

I was hungry, but the committee man who had led us here said we must find our own food. We could cook outdoors and use the school toilets.

There were half-rotten apples and orange peels in my rucksack.

"Wait," Ko said, "don't eat them." She took me outside. "Find some rocks." In a small circle of rocks she built a fire, cut the good part of the apples in small pieces, added water, and cooked them in the two mess kits. She put the fire out carefully when the apples were cooked.

"Our first meal in the homeland," she said, acting cheerful, as she took the food inside. She poured a large portion into Mother's wooden rice bowl. "And, the first hot meal since we had that roasted corn." She divided the remainder.

Mother held the bowl and gazed at it for a long time. The apple water steamed. She shook her head gently and shock was in her voice. "These bowls and the few belongings we have here are the only mementos from our beloved home." Slowly she brought the bowl to her lips.

For the first night in my homeland we spread two blankets beneath us, snuggled together, and covered ourselves with Mother's large blanket. My blanket, once fleecy white, was gray, dusty, and stained with blood. I knew I could sleep in peace, without the sound of airplanes or the danger of being bombed, attacked, or raped, but often during the night I jerked awake and sat up in fear that someone might attack me or steal our belongings. When I had to go to the toilet I woke Ko, frightened that men were hiding there.

Mother went alone to the post office next day to wire my grandparents in Aomori that we had arrived. Two days later the message was returned, care of the refugee camp. Unable to deliver.

Mother began to worry. What had happened to her parents? Ko suggested that we leave at once for her hometown, Aomori.

"No, I cannot go without Hideyo," Mother said. "Now that we are safely here all I think of is Hideyo." Her voice trembled into tears.

It was strange we did not think more of Father, whom we loved dearly. But he was so far away and probably, we knew, now in the hands of the Russians, who had won the war. We prayed that somewhere he was safe.

Every day we rolled our blankets and, carrying our loads, walked the long distance back to the shipyard to ask if any Korean fishing boats had arrived, and if anyone had seen Hideyo. Over and over Mother described him. Week after week the ship that had brought us came back from Korea with another hundred refugees—but no Hideyo.

It was November. We had been at the refugee camp over a month and we were told that we must leave, to make room for newcomers.

"Please, another week!" Mother begged. "We are waiting for my son." He might be dead by now, she was told. We were taking needed room.

"Let's leave today," said Ko. "I won't stand such treatment."

She went alone to the shipyard and left a message at the office to tell Hideyo we were going to Aomori at the northern tip of Honshu. The office gave her three train tickets.

I was surprised to see how much smaller Japanese trains were than the ones I was used to in Korea. We were able to get into third class, but it was packed with refugees and discharged soldiers. The aisles were filled with standees, and young men hung from the sides of the cars. On top of the train people clung together like grapes on the vine.

The train smelled of rotten fish. Ko whispered that many would get off as the train stopped at stations and we would find space to sit. She didn't think she could stand all the way. But as for me, the thought of meeting my grandparents so excited me that I decided no matter how tired or hungry I became I would not complain.

Then, as the train jolted along, Mother announced that we would get off at Kyoto.

Ko and I cried together. "We're not going to Grandmother's?"

"I've thought about it over and over," said Mother. "You must get back to school and Kyoto is the only town that escaped bombing."

"No," Ko protested, "let us go north with you. School can wait. We've only missed it for three months and a few more days won't matter."

But Mother shook her head. Kyoto was the place where she had received a cultural education when she was young. It had much to offer.

"Is there anyone there we know?" Ko asked. "Where can we stay?"

"We'll find a place to stay. Your education comes first," Mother told her. "As soon as I settle you girls I'll go north and find out what has happened."

"I don't want to go to school," I said. "I want to go with you." Mother closed her eyes and did not answer.

Instead of many people getting off the train, more got on, and we were pushed and squeezed. Again and again my wounded chest was hurt, and I put my hand over the sore spot automatically to protect it. Ko leaned against the wooden panel of a toilet, Mother leaned on Ko, and I leaned on Mother.

Three days on the train. No food. My stomach ached with emptiness and thirst. There was not even space to take my rucksack from my back. I asked Mother to open the flap and find just anything. She handed me some orange peels, and though they were dry they had a sweet, tart taste. I chewed and chewed and swallowed. Mother and Ko did the same.

I thought my legs had turned to a pair of sticks and that I could not stand much more. So when the train pulled into the Kyoto station I moved with vast relief.

In the station we found a spot. Ko scouted and said there was a public well outside the buildings, and she stayed while Mother and I went for a drink. As I scooped water from the well pool, the western sky, fiery red, was reflected in the water. I suddenly thought of Hideyo. Would he ever find us? Or was he really dead? I began to cry.

Mother asked what was wrong. I did not want to mention Hideyo so I said, "I won't like this city. I want to go with you!"

"You must learn to take likes and dislikes in this world," Mother told me, drying my wet face. "I will be back and I promise never to leave you alone again."

We used our usual techniques in the station, finding good spots, taking turns sleeping and watching our belongings. These were now our only possessions in the world.

Ko was at the well, washing and rinsing some clothes, when I woke the next morning. I stepped out of the station to join her and found heavy frost on the ground. I wet my inch-long hair, trying in vain to make it lie down.

"Look!" Ko cried. "A streetcar!"

I had never seen a streetcar, and I stood still in amazement. A few people got off or on the car and then it moved on, bells chiming. The people who had got off were walking briskly into the station. They wore beautiful clothes. They passed by us.

"Going to work, I suppose," said Ko.

That was a different world. Here in the station there were refugees, beggars, wounded soldiers, pickpockets, orphans, and prostitutes, making this their home. A few feet away people in decent clothes were going peacefully to work, with homes to go back to.

Mother, wearing her national clothes, dusted off her shoes and went to the city hall to inquire about schools. She took the small pouch from her chemise pocket and gave Ko ten yen (about three cents). Three hundred and sixty yen were a dollar. She said that if we saw a man pushing a food cart to buy something to eat. She asked a policeman at the exit for directions and he pointed. She bowed slightly and went.

"Mother is getting terribly thin," said Ko. "Let's surprise her with lots of food."

The Station Hotel stood about four blocks away, and, carrying our loads, we found an alley behind the building. There was cooked rice in the big garbage cans, half-eaten roasted fish, pickles, and seaweed. We packed our mess kits full and hurried back to the station. Mother came back, very tired. We found a bench and opened our kits.

"I have learned about good schools," Mother said. "I'll take you there tomorrow."

"I have no clothes!" I protested. "And look at my shoe, ripped open. I don't want to go to school!"

I was going to school, she told me, to learn and to become an educated person. I did not need to decorate myself.

Ko was busy the rest of the day. She aired the thin summer trousers and blouse I had worn when I left Nanam. She washed my head, and I tried again to flatten my hair, but it stood up as soon as it dried and I looked like a porcupine. Ko washed my back, reaching under my blouse, at the well. She told me to crawl under the bench and get some sleep, as my day would start early. I went to sleep wearing my overcoat and the soldier's clothes and wrapped in my blanket, hoping tomorrow would never come and send me to school.

Mother woke me early, and Ko made me wash and put on my Nanam clothes. Mother did a strange thing. She emptied her big wrapping cloth and took the cloth with her to the toilet. Then she came back and told Ko to put back all the humble items. Ko wished me luck, and Mother and I headed for the streetcar stop.

Though I did not want to go to school, riding on the streetcar fascinated me. I watched the city scene from the window, and Mother pointed out ancient buildings and a castle and explained what they were.

"You will like it here," she assured me.

The two-story Sagano Girls' School stood at the foot of Atago Mountain, surrounded by camellias and bamboo trees. We crossed the frosty ground. My heart beat loudly as I sat next to Mother in the principal's office. My head was full of questions. Would they take me? Would the girls like me? Be nice to me? Through a glass door I could see well-dressed girls with bright bags, and then I looked down at my shabby trousers and shoes, the left one tied with a piece of the same rope Mother had used, so long ago, to tie my wrist.

The school clerk, also well-dressed, brought Mother a tea tray and bowed. As she left she glanced at my head and almost smiled. I knew I looked funny, and again I stroked my head to make that hair lie down, in vain.

"Good morning." A man had come in. "I am Mr. Ishida, the principal."

Mother and I stood and bowed deeply, and my knees began to shake. Mother introduced us and asked if the school would accept me. "My daughter has been out of school since July." She handed him my report sheets from Nanam that gave my parents' names, father's occupation, family status, and my grades.

The principal studied the sheet. From somewhere I heard the chorus of "Blue Danube." If they won't take me, I thought, I can go north with Mother. She wouldn't leave me at the station alone when Ko was in school. I began to hope they wouldn't take me.

Suddenly the principal looked at Mother, and then at me.

He said in amazement, "You survived!"

"We did." Mother's voice was low.

"And your husband?"

"We do not know. He was in Manchuria for the government when we fled." I was glad he did not ask about Hideyo because I knew Mother would break down right there.

"We shall be happy to accept your daughter," the principal said. "I am sure she can catch up. The tuition is thirty yen a month and you must buy your own books and supplies. You may arrange all that with the clerk." He sent for a Miss Asada.

Miss Asada was a pretty lady dressed in a dark blue suit and a white blouse. She studied my report sheet and nodded. "Our school system is different from Korea's," she said. "I would like to give Miss Yoko some tests." She led me to a desk and gave me paper and a pencil. While Mother talked to the principal I went to work on the papers: mathematics, national language, sentence construction, and a mental test of character.

I saw Mother bowing to the principal. "Don't go!" I begged.

"I must take your sister to school." She handed me three yen for carfare.

"I don't know how to get back!"

"Take streetcar number three." She bowed again, opened the office door, and silently closed it. My eyes followed her elegant walk until she disappeared. Suddenly I felt defenseless and abandoned, and I could not stop the tears. I made a fist of my left hand and bit my thumb as hard as I could, to fight my loneliness for Mother and Ko.

I made tear spots on the work papers and finished them, sniffing and wiping away tears with my sleeves, as I did not own a handkerchief. I handed the papers to the principal, and Miss Asada came back to look over my work.

"Very good." She gave me a smile. Both she and

Mr. Ishida seemed friendly, and I decided I liked this school. When the principal gave me a student's handbook I liked him even more. Then Miss Asada and I walked to the classroom.

I could hear the students talking as we went down the hall, but when Miss Asada opened the door there was sudden silence. Thirty girls stared at me. No teacher was in sight.

"Everyone," said Miss Asada, "this is Miss Kawashima Yoko." In Japan everyone is officially called by the family name.

I bowed deeply, but instead of return bows everyone began to laugh. The laughter went on. My hair, I thought. I tried to lay it flat.

Miss Asada spoke firmly. "Silence! Miss Kawashima has just returned from Korea. She is a good student and I expect you to be helpful to her as she becomes used to this school."

She turned to me. "For your cleaning assignment today you will be part of the group that does this room." Then she placed me in a back seat. I felt desperately unhappy and out of place with these girls in their fine clothes. All had long hair, some in braids.

Then a man teacher came in, a history teacher, it turned out. I had no books, no pencil or paper, but I listened. Loneliness attacked me again and I sniffed back tears. I could not wait for school to be over so that I could get back to the station, where I belonged, with Mother and Ko.

After class, I had to linger for my cleaning assignment. Some of the girls, as they went out, tossed papers into a wastepaper basket. This gave me an idea and I examined the basket. The papers were crumpled, but many had little writing and all were blank on one side. I picked them up and smoothed the wrinkled sheets. I looked for a pencil too, but there was none.

"You want more paper?" a girl asked. She made an airplane with a piece of notebook paper and aimed at me. The others laughed. I bit my lip, but I did not shed tears when it flew, for collecting papers was a lot easier than looking for food in trash cans. Trying to ignore the girls, I unfolded the airplane and smoothed the wrinkles.

There were six of us left to do the cleaning assignment. I had no dustcloth so I asked a girl with a broom if I could sweep, and she shoved the broom at me and walked off. As I swept and came near the girls who were dusting, they scattered, as if I were carrying contagion.

If they had gone through what we had experienced, I thought, they would be compassionate. They just don't know! Tears came again as I swept. I longed not only for Mother and Ko but for Father and Hideyo.

Then a middle-aged man came in pushing a large cart. He saw the almost empty trash basket. He spoke, stuttering. "N-n-no t-t-t-trash?"

A girl imitated him. "W-w-we h-h-have a n-n-new t-t-t-trash girl." She pointed at me. The girls thought this was very funny.

The man gave me a glance and went away. I ran to the next classroom after him. I remembered Father saying once that he had helped to cure a stuttering classmate by talking very slowly with him. I spoke slowly. "Are you going to burn all these papers?" He nodded. "I need papers badly and some pencils. Please let me go through all the trash."

"S-s-s-sure. C-c-come to the f-f-f-furnace r-r-r-room."

Again I spoke very slowly. "It is my first day. Where is the furnace room?"

He told me. In the furnace room, waiting to be burned, I found plenty of usable paper, some short pencils, and even erasers. I gathered them all. Honorable Sister would be glad to have these. I thanked the man and at last dashed outdoors toward the streetcar stop.

On the streetcar I wrote down as much as I could remember of the history and geography lessons. If I only had books! I decided to ask Miss Asada to lend me books until I could get my own at some second-hand store.

The familiar Kyoto station came in sight and I jumped off, the bundle of papers in my arms. Mother was on the concrete floor of the station watching our belongings. She smiled at me. "How did it go?"

"The girls were very snobbish, but I liked the lessons."

"You will find all kinds of people in this world," she told me. "You will learn to handle them. Just do not lose your good values."

"Where is Honorable Sister?"

"She's not home yet. She went to school by herself so I could rest."

I showed Mother my papers and pencils from the furnace room and she laughed. "Our lives will be better when Father returns," she told me. "For now we must just endure. We can endure anything now after what we have been through. Right?"

I said, "Right!"

Ko, it turned out, had passed entrance tests and been admitted to the University. She was delighted with my paper and pencils. I asked how her day had gone, thinking bitterly of the laughter and scorn I had experienced.

"Fine," she said.

"Didn't they laugh at you?"

"They did."

"What did you do?"

"Nothing. They have a lot to learn. I showed them how good I am at the academic work."

We studied that day on the station floor. Mother watched the benches and seized a vacancy when she saw one, calling us to come. So now we had space, and food, from the garbage cans, was no problem. Our tuition was paid for six months. Mother said she would take the early train north.

How would she pay for the train, I wondered, for I knew she had little cash and no savings book. Ko wondered too. "I hope you didn't sell yourself on the street yesterday?" she asked Mother, teasing.

Mother laughed. "No, I brought some cash from Korea. Don't worry. Just study hard, for me."

We got up extra early to see her off. She gave Ko some money for school supplies and for a cake of soap and toothbrushes and the streetcar fare, half price for students. "I'll be back next Friday," she called as the train pulled out.

Chapter 8

Ko rearranged our rucksacks. In my rucksack she put all the papers and in hers the mess kits, five canteens, eating utensils, matches, and candles. She gave me both of these to carry while she toted the huge wrapping cloth bundle. "Well, let's go to school," she said. "We'll meet right here beneath the station clock."

When I entered the classroom a girl called out, "You brought two rucksacks for the trash?"

This time I talked back. "What's wrong with that?"

Everyone laughed. I remembered what Ko had said and decided to pay no attention, but deep inside I wanted to beat that girl up.

The trash man had not burned the trash when I showed up after school. I conversed with him, very slowly. I told him Kyoto was much warmer than northern Korea. He asked about Nanam. I was speaking so slowly that our conversation took a long time, but he seemed to enjoy it and for the first time I saw him smile.

A few days later when I ran to the furnace room he was not there. I was busy picking out papers when he tapped me on the back. "S-s-s-saved th-th-them f-f-for you f-f-from t-t-t-trash. Th-th-thought y-y-you c-can u-u-use them." He handed me a compass, scissors, a slide rule, and a dictionary!

"Oh, thank you very much!" I spoke so slowly. "Now I have to make a good grade!"

"Y-y-you are fine g-girl!" he said.

I noticed that the words "are fine" had come smoothly from his lips. "I will see you tomorrow," I said, wanting to hear his response.

"*Sayonara,*" he said, very slowly but smoothly.

"*Sayonara!*" I answered in the same way.

All the way to the station my heart was skipping and hopping with happiness. Not only did I have a friend, but he was speaking almost normally. I couldn't wait to tell Ko. Father was right. If everyone would speak to that man slowly he would get over his stuttering.

On my fifth morning, as I entered the classroom, all the girls were gathered at the bulletin board. I went to see what they were looking at, and they scattered as they saw me with my two rucksacks. On the board was a huge drawing of me with my rucksacks, picking up trash in the furnace room. Under the drawing was writing. "Democratic System! Prestigious Sagano Accepts Trash-Picker as Student."

This did it. I would not spend another day in this class. Then there was a shout. The trash man. "God-damn girls!" he yelled, and he did not stutter. He pulled off the drawing and tore it to pieces. "Go to your class," he told me, and still he spoke smoothly. And in spite of my anguish I smiled at him, I was so happy at the way he spoke. "Keep smiling," he said, and went away.

I managed the classes that day. In the furnace room I stayed a little longer to talk with my friend, as this was to be my last day.

Riding back to the station, I wondered how I was going to tell Ko that I would not go to school anymore. I was glad she was not waiting under the clock. It was five o'clock and a train pulled in, letting off many commuters on their way home. How I envied them. I have no home, I thought, no father, no brother, and right now no mother. Just a big sister who is strong and rough and sometimes very bossy.

Still, she loves me. When we did not find much food in the garbage she gave me most of it, saying my little dumb brain would not function without food and winter winds would blow me away.

Ko was coming now, walking fast and carrying our heaviest bundle. She leaned forward as she walked, and I thought she looked just like Father. He always looked down, thinking, as he strolled in the garden.

Ko spotted me. "Have you waited long? Let's go get some food."

As we walked toward the alley for our supper and breakfast supplies, I still did not know how to tell her. "I've had an idea," Ko said. "I'll be coming back to the station a couple of hours later now. So you do your homework and I'll get our food on my way home. That will save time."

"What's your idea? Why are you going to be late?" I asked.

"I have things to do at school. Don't ask questions."

I could not tell her my decision. And I dragged myself back to school. Somehow the days passed, and I endured.

Then it was Friday and Mother would be back. I asked Ko if I could skip school. "No," she said. "School is paid for and you can't waste a day."

I could hardly wait for school to be over. No matter what scorn was poured on me, the thought of Mother made me so happy I seemed to be walking all day on silky clouds. I ran to the furnace room to gather my papers. I ran to the streetcar. The car was not running fast enough. I ran to the station building, my eyes seeking Mother.

She was there, sitting alone, caped with her blanket. She looked lonesome and so tiny.

"Welcome back!" I called, running. "I missed you!"

She looked up and smiled. How pale she was, her lips white. "I missed you too, terribly!"

I squeezed in between her and a lady next to her. "Are you all right?" I asked.

"A bit dizzy. Tired, I guess." She was breathing hard.

"How are our grandparents?"

Mother shook her head weakly. "Destroyed— everything gone." She paused. "My parents and your father's parents were all killed in the July bombing."

I could hardly take it in. "What," I said slowly, "are we going to do now?" I had thought we would go to Grandmother's and be cared for.

"I don't know." She seemed to breathe with difficulty. "I put up our land for sale, and I left your sister's school address at the town hall if—if they hear from Hideyo or Father." She was crying. "Isn't your sister late?" She closed her eyes.

The lady got up and I slid over to give Mother more room. She lay down and put her head in my lap. "Wake me when your sister comes."

Suddenly I felt grown-up. Suddenly I knew I must protect Mother. I wiggled out of my overcoat and covered her slender shoulders. Ko was carrying the blankets in the wrapping cloth. Why didn't she come!

"Little One," Mother said, "I'm thirsty."

I pulled out a canteen and flew to the well. Mother is ill, Mother is ill! I dunked the whole canteen in the well, wanting it to fill fast. I raced back.

She raised her head and drank. "Ah, thanks. It tastes good." She lay down again. "I wish Ko would come." She was panting.

"She'll come, she'll come," I told her. "She is getting us some food." My eyes searched the crowd of people streaming through the station, wishing that Ko had not had that idea, whatever it was, that kept her two hours.

Mother was speaking, her voice faint. "Little One, is she coming?"

"Any minute, Honorable Mother."

"Hang on—hang on to the—wrapping cloth. Hang on . . ." Mother's head slipped to one side, and her right arm dropped, and she was still.

I knew. I screamed. "Mother! She is gone! Mother is gone!" I kept on screaming and crying.

People gathered around us and the police took my name and asked questions—Mother's name, her age, her hometown. The doctor had come, to pronounce Mother dead, when Ko finally arrived. She could not believe it. What had happened? What had Mother been doing? What had she said? I answered, sobbing, and told her how much Mother had wanted to see her. "I wished you were not staying in school those extra hours!"

Ko knelt beside Mother. She pushed back Mother's hair. She bit her lips tightly and tried not to show tears but she could not hold them back. Then she burst out. "You made it all the way from Nanam! Why now? Why now?" She threw herself over Mother and wept. Then she grabbed a mess kit full of food and slammed it down on the concrete floor. The lid burst open and the food scattered. Bystanders, beggars, orphans, station dwellers, quickly squatted down to feast.

The police telephoned a funeral service and two men came. They asked Ko what type of casket we wanted. Ko said we had no money, but was there some way we could cremate the body? They said they could put the body on a pine board and take it to a crematorium.

"How much?" Ko asked.

"Twenty yen, in advance."

Ko looked in Mother's pouch and counted bills,

trying not to let the money be seen. Somehow I did not like the attitude of the two men and I told Ko in Korean that they might be cheating us. Ko nodded.

"Twenty yen is too high," Ko said. "A pine board doesn't cost that much."

"Gasoline and use of the truck," said the man. "The truck consumes much gas and oil."

"How far to the crematorium?"

"Very far, about an hour and half."

Ko was figuring. "What kind of truck do you have?"

"A Datsun."

"A Datsun doesn't consume much gas and oil. Twenty yen is too high."

"Are you gonna pay us in advance or not?" the man asked.

"You bring your truck with the pine board. Deliver us to the crematorium and I'll pay you."

"No way," said the funeral service man.

"Well, I'll just have to call the city hall," said Ko. "They'll help us for free."

The men headed for the exit but one returned. "We'll take you to the crematorium," he said.

The policeman chased all the people around us away and he stayed near us. Ko and I wiped Mother's face with a damp cloth and combed her hair for our farewell. We were both sobbing. Mother was wearing her wartime national clothes, and Ko checked all the hidden pockets. She found some bills and coins, also Mother's identification slip showing that she was a refugee from Korea. I put them in my rucksack. Then Ko drew the precious sword from between Mother's breasts and slipped it against her own chest. She checked Mother's socks. There was a hole in one and she slipped it off and put on one of her own. Then she brought Mother's hands together against her breasts.

It was then that a lady approached us. She was not a station dweller, but she was a familiar face for she came to the station every day. We had never spoken to each other.

"I am Mrs. Masuda," she introduced herself. "I am sorry about your mother. Is there anything I can do to help you?"

"We are waiting for the truck," Ko told her.

"May I come with you to the crematorium?" asked Mrs. Masuda. "I have been watching you ever since you arrived. I wondered where your mother went."

"She went north to settle a few things," Ko answered. "Mother would be glad if you would come with us."

"There is a crematorium very near here," Mrs. Masuda told Ko. "You do not have to ride for an hour and a half."

"But aren't you waiting for someone?" Ko asked.

"I have been waiting for my niece from Seoul, but she was not on the last train. I am on my way home."

When the truck came the men lifted Mother to the board and slid it onto the pickup. Ko and I threw in our belongings and jumped on. Mrs. Masuda ordered the driver to go to Higashiyama Crematory, only a twenty-minute drive, and when we arrived there she paid five yen to the driver.

The man in charge at the crematorium was kind. He and his helpers carried Mother, on the board, and slid it carefully into the mouth the furnace. Cremation is different in Japan. We were told we could light the fire if we wished. I cried and held on to Mrs. Masuda, but Ko courageously lit the fire at the mouth of the furnace. The flame spread quickly. I could not look.

"She will be ready in the morning," said the man. "You may select an urn now." But Ko said we would bring an urn for our beloved mother.

Ko, Mrs. Masuda, and I walked back to the station. As I went down the hill I looked back. Twilight was fading and the smoke rose slowly, spreading into the sky. Ko carried the wrapping cloth bundle, I carried the two rucksacks, and Mrs. Masuda held my hand as we walked, wordless.

Mrs. Masuda broke the silence. "Do you have a place to go?"

"No," said Ko, "but my little sister and I would like to stay in the city for six months." She explained about school.

Mrs. Masuda told us that she and her husband owned a small *geta* (clog) factory on the west side of town, and their warehouse had been robbed. She would be delighted if we would go there to stay and watch things. "Your schools would be much closer," she said.

Ko thanked her and said we would like to go tomorrow after we claimed Mother's ashes. "Then I shall go to the station to meet you," our new friend said.

Strangely, this offer of a home did not excite us much. In our grief nothing else seemed to matter, and it had begun to seem normal to live in stations.

We did not sleep that night. Morning was bright. Ko told me to wash Mother's mess kit and dry it well. "It will be Mother's urn," she said. When the clock struck nine we carried our belongings and headed toward the crematorium.

As I said, cremation is different in Japan, and not all of the body was destroyed. With chopsticks brought all the way from Nanam we gently placed the small remains of Mother's bones in her mess kit. I sobbed. Oh, Mother! Then Ko paid the price for cremation and we carried the mess-kit urn away.

On the way to the station we stopped at a small temple and asked a monk to say a prayer for our dead. But the monk, wrapped in his sacred black and white daily robes, stared at us and said sharply, "I have no time." He slammed the *fusuma* (panel) and vanished.

I held Mother's urn close to my breast. "Damn monk!" Ko shouted. "A Buddhist monk should practice nothing but love. He is doing a fine job!"

I made up my mind that I would never step into a Buddhist temple as long as I lived.

Mrs. Masuda took us to the warehouse. It was beside the streetcar tracks. A path connected it with the factory and a stream ran behind it. Upstairs was a four-*tatami*-mat room with a small window and a bare light bulb hanging from the ceiling. She said we could cook outside and use all the scraps of wood from the factory. "The room has not been cleaned for ages," she said, and she lent us a broom and bucket and rags.

Ko and I went to work. We removed cobwebs from corners. I washed the window while Ko swept the mats and wiped them with a damp cloth. We scrubbed the stairway and swept the entrance. When we had finished we went to the stream to wash our hands and faces.

Then we made a simple altar for Mother in our room. We folded her bath towel and rested the mess-kit urn on it. While I filled Mother's canteen at the stream, Ko broke small branches from a bright maple tree and we arranged them in the canteen. Together we offered it on Mother's altar. Then Ko placed Mother's short sword in front of the urn and we bowed deeply to Mother's ashes. I asked her to watch over Ko and me.

Chapter 9

Ko grieved that she had not returned to the station before Mother went. "If I had only been thirty minutes earlier!" she said, sobbing.

"Your smart idea was not that smart," I said, crying myself and remembering how my eyes had searched the crowd for Ko. Then I said as an afterthought, "Mother told me to hang on to the wrapping cloth."

"Naturally. It contains all our underwear, extra clothes, and papers," Ko said. "They're more important than our rucksacks."

"But she didn't sound as if she meant that." I remembered how she had told me to *hang on . . . hang on*. "I think she meant the cloth itself was important."

But now in her grief this was not important to Ko. "Are you hungry?" she asked.

"More tired than hungry," I said, and lay down on the tatami mat. Although the straw mat was old and smelled musty it felt good on my back. The tiny room had only four mats but it protected us from wind and from thieves. Tomorrow is Sunday, I thought. I can sleep to my heart's content.

"Do you know what I miss in the station?" asked Ko.

"What?" I was startled that Ko could actually miss those horrible surroundings.

"The clock. I don't know what time it is now," she replied. "It's getting dark and cold."

"And I am going to sleep," I said, because I did not

want to be reminded of the sadness at the station.

I spread one blanket on the floor and covered myself with two. Ko came into the blankets. She cuddled close to me and remarked that the room was much colder than the station because of drafts from downstairs.

"But we can sleep without worrying about thieves or being attacked," I said, earnestly wishing she would never again bring up the word "station."

I could not help going over and over the way Mother had died and her last words. In the darkness I faced Mother's mess-kit urn and hoped it would speak to me. I tossed and turned.

"What's wrong?" asked Ko.

"I can't sleep."

"I thought you were tired."

"Mother's last words haunt me."

"She only meant to hang on to all we have in the cloth," said Ko. "Now let's sleep. I'll cook you something good tomorrow."

I persisted. "Answer this question. Every time Mother went to the toilet to change she took the wrapping cloth with her. Remember, she emptied everything from the cloth that time before she went to the toilet and made you put everything in again when she returned."

"Because she had a unique way of taking off her underpants and putting her trousers back on. She used the cloth as a hip wrapper."

"In the small toilet with the door locked?" I said.

"You never know about locks in public toilets. Besides, she was old-fashioned." Again Ko snuggled against me. She felt warm and soon, as my cold body warmed, I went to sleep.

I woke when a streetcar passed, giving a long whistle, and shook the warehouse. It was dawn. Ko was snoring and I lay still. What would she fix us for breakfast, I wondered. Hot rice and soup with lots of fresh tofu and green onions in it would be a great treat. Mrs. Masuda had paid for the funeral truck, so Ko had that twenty yen. I hope she'll use it today for food, I thought. The more I thought about good food the hungrier I got. I wished Ko would wake up.

When I turned I faced Mother's altar and again her last words came back. I'm going to investigate that wrapping cloth, I thought, and slipped quietly out from the blanket.

"What are you doing?" Ko asked. "It's Sunday. Let's sleep."

"I'm going to check the wrapping cloth."

"Do it later."

But I could not sleep anymore. I crawled over to the wrapping bundle. It was a soft canvaslike material, double, and Ko had tied it so tightly I could not undo the knot.

"Honorable Sister! Please wake up."

"I am awake."

"Untie the knot and then I won't bother you."

She grumbled that I gave her no peace, but she untied the knot. I pulled out our socks, underwear, extra trousers, and blouses. At the bottom were the insurance papers, birth certificates, report sheets, and Father's name seal. In Japan working people carry name seals, in jade or ivory perhaps, to stamp their names on papers. Father's seal was jade.

"See, Little One. Mother meant these are the important things," said Ko, picking up the seal. "This is very important. Maybe Mother wanted us to collect some insurance." She looked at the policies, but somehow we both knew any insurance was valueless now.

"Now put everything back."

She crawled into the blankets again and I put the papers back, then folded our humble garments neatly. I took one corner of the cloth and folded it over. The opposite corner felt heavier and stiff, and I heard paper slipping down somewhere between the two layers of cloth.

"Honorable Sister, get up!" I said. I stood up and turned on the light.

"Now what?" said Ko.

"Something is between the layers."

Ko sat up then. She removed everything from the wrapping cloth and examined the seam carefully. At the corner of the cloth where I had felt stiffness was a zipper. Ko opened it and the cloth separated to two pieces. Here was a square pocket.

Ko had known of the other pockets but not this one. She pulled out thousand-yen and hundred-yen bills one after the other, then Hideyo's, Ko's, and my savings books. But the money had been drawn out on July 15, two weeks before we fled.

Now I understood why Mother had taken the wrapper to the toilet every time. She did not need to change, she needed money.

Ko counted a little over thirty-six thousand yen—a hundred dollars. We looked at each other in amazement. "Mother said she brought some cash from Korea," Ko said. "This is where she hid it."

She put back all the money. We were not going to use that money, she said. It would be for emergencies only—for when we became ill and had to pay a doctor. She instructed me to be sure and grab the wrapping bundle in case of fire.

"Let's go outdoors and wash," Ko said, folding the top blanket. The soft sunlight beamed through the window and felt warm on my back.

The water was icy, but we washed. Walking back

around the factory building, we discovered an old abandoned fruit box that would make an excellent cupboard-table combination and also could be our study desk. We washed it and tipped it against our stairway to dry. There was a water faucet outside the warehouse and we filled our five canteens.

Although it was Sunday I heard people in the factory. The door was open and I saw Mrs. Masuda. She waved to us to come in. She was talking to a man on crutches, her husband, and she introduced us.

We bowed deeply to him to show our appreciation of their letting us stay in the warehouse.

"I've heard about you girls," Mr. Masuda said. "Did you sleep well? Were you afraid?"

"No," I answered. "But I woke up when a streetcar passed."

"That's the first car. Five-thirty," he said. "It wakes me too."

"If you girls need some pots," said Mrs. Masuda, "I have some old ones. We live right over there." She pointed across the tracks.

"Oh, thank you," said Ko. "And is there a grocery near by?"

Mrs. Masuda said the general store was half a mile to the east, and we walked there. Ko bought four cups of rice, half a pound of *miso* (bean paste), and one cake of fresh tofu. My mouth was already watering. She bought needles, thread, a razor blade, and a bar of laundry soap too.

"What are you going to do with the razor blade?" I asked.

"After breakfast you are going to rip the soldiers' uniforms apart, so I can make you a winter coat," she replied.

She built a fire outside the warehouse and I went to borrow two cooking pots. Ko cooked a cup of rice and made miso soup. Just as I had dreamed, but with no green onion. It was the only decent breakfast we had had in almost five months.

"Eat slowly. Chew well," said Ko. "What's left will be our supper."

She carried the utensils to the stream to wash them, and I sat against the sunny wall of the warehouse ripping the uniforms. As I clipped with the sharp blade I shivered, thinking of what would have happened to us if the airplane had not dropped a bomb and killed the Korean Communist soldiers. A fraction of a moment, I thought, had been the difference between life and death. The three uniforms became pieces and bits. I took them to the stream, rubbed the bar of soap on each piece, and pounded them with a wooden stick I had borrowed from a factory worker. I pounded especially where the material was stained with blood, trying hard to forget the ordeal we had gone through.

The workers in the factory listened to the radio as they worked, and I also noticed the factory had a small wall clock. They worked from eight to four. So we could guess what time it was. I got up by the first streetcar, and when Mr. Masuda closed the factory it was four-thirty. The last streetcar came by at twelve-thirty.

As the days rolled into December the frost grew heavier. I wore my summer trousers and blouse and my little red overcoat from Nanam, as Ko had not finished my overcoat from the soldiers' uniforms.

When the first snow came I caped myself with my blanket. As I entered the classroom sixty eyes stared at me. I stared back. One girl said, "Rag doll! Aren't you ashamed to come to school like that?"

"Ashamed of what?" I said firmly. "My tuition is paid. I have the right to come to this school." I folded my blanket over the back of my chair, took out my English reader and began reading the sentences.

"Trash Picker and Rag Doll are good names for her," another said. Then Mr. Yoshida came in and there was silence. They always stopped when the teacher appeared, and I was too proud to tell the teacher how they were treating me.

I wanted to scream at the whole class, to tell them they were stupid and had much to learn about life and death. I had a hard time controlling myself. I will show them how good I am at academic work. I will beat every one of them with my grades, I thought. The grades are the only weapon I have now.

Though I was terribly unhappy in the classroom, it was my joy to go to the furnace room and talk with the stuttering man, Mr. Naido. He was the only friend I had in the school. He saved for me books, glue, art pencils, crayons, India ink, and calligraphy brushes. I learned, while talking with him and picking up papers, that because of his speech handicap he had not been accepted in the Japanese navy. He had had a hard time finding a job as he had only a primary education. He had finally found this job.

"Because," he said, "all the men were killed or wounded and the school could not find a normal-speaking person." Whenever Mr. Naido talked with me he stuttered less and less, which made me very happy. Maybe Father can cure him completely when he comes, I thought.

"If my father comes home safely," I said, smiling at him, "will you meet him? He is a fine man and fun."

"He will come home. He must come home." He patted my back.

Mr. Naido had been on my side ever since I came to this school and I did not know how to thank him, but I decided that at the end of the term I would show him report sheets that said straight A plus!

As I left the furnace room one day I noticed a cart full of cans and empty bottles. What was he doing with them? I asked.

"I sell them," he said. "The girls are very wasteful. Most of their fathers are prestigious and the girls are badly spoiled."

"If I bring some cans will you sell them for me?" I asked.

"Bring cans anytime," he said, slowly but without stuttering.

So, my walking posture changed. I developed the habit of looking down when I walked, to search for cans and bottles. Whenever I found one I put it in Ko's rucksack and took it to Mr. Naido.

The price of everything had tripled. Ko and I continued to live poorly, for Ko would not touch Mother's hidden money.

She was doing well at Seian University, majoring in home economics. The professors liked Ko's sewing, and often they handed her kimonos to make for department stores. She did especially well designing women's western garments.

The department stores did not want leftover material, so Ko kept it. She made babies' and toddlers' clothes and children's play items. These she gave to me to sell from door to door on my way home from school.

"You can have that money," she said. "Buy yourself a pair of shoes."

For a pair of shoes I worked hard to sell the items Ko made. Whatever I earned I placed beneath Mother's urn. I felt secure with Mother watching my earnings.

Ko began asking her classmates to save all their

scraps. From them she made beanbags for girls, the traditional New Year's toy. She showed me how to make them too and said I should make a couple of them each night when I had finished my homework.

Because New Year's was coming many families with little girls wanted to buy beanbags, and I wanted a new pair of shoes badly. When I had enough bags I went to this house and that house one afternoon to sell. Then I walked home on the car tracks, jumping aside when a car approached. Whenever I came to a station and saw a newspaper flapping on a bench I picked it up for fuel.

Ko was already home and had waited supper for me. "What took you so long? I was worried."

"I sold everything," I said happily, and placed the money under Mother's urn.

"You must come home before dark," said Ko. "I don't want you wandering around."

I talked back. "I was not wandering. I want a pair of shoes!"

"Your safety is more important than shoes," Ko said. "Let's eat."

As we ate Ko happened to cast her eyes on the front page of the newspaper. She stopped eating and picked up the paper to read. She said the government had just opened a new port, Maizuru, for refugees arriving from Korea and Manchuria. Also the government had been negotiating with Russia to let the remaining Japanese come home.

"The port of Fukuoka, where we landed, will be closed this week," said Ko. "They'll move the refugee center to Maizuru and that's only an hour's ride from here. Let's go this weekend and make some investigations about Father and Hideyo."

Another piece of good news she read to me was that the government would give refugees futons as a

New Year's gift.

Ko beamed. "Now Mr. Prime Minister Yoshida is really talking! All we have to do is take our refugee certificates to the city hall. Let's do it Friday afternoon."

Thinking of sleeping between futon and comforters excited me and I could hardly wait for Friday to come. Ko borrowed two long ropes from Mr. Masuda to tie the futons, and we took a streetcar.

She showed our refugee papers and Mother's at the small window. "Three of you?" asked the man. "Where is the third?"

"Mother could not come," answered Ko.

He stamped the certificates, and in a back room a lady handed us the futons. Ko tied a rope around one set, cotton-filled mattress and comforter, and put it on my back. They were so heavy that I staggered. Ko carried the other two sets.

While waiting for the streetcar I asked her why she had taken Mother's certificate. She said she had not registered Mother's death, so that as far as Kyoto City was concerned Mother was still alive. "We must have extra bedding for Honorable Father or Hideyo."

The bedding was a load on my back and the rope dug in where I was wounded, but I did not complain, for the joy of sleeping in bed like everybody else made me all excited.

I couldn't wait to make our beds and to lie down and feel what it was to sleep on a futon. Though this bedding was not nearly as fine as the bedding we had slept in in Korea, we were most appreciative, for we had really shivered at night with no heat in the warehouse.

Ko and I stayed up late that night, sewing. She made little clothes and I made small cloth dolls and beanbags. When they were done I turned to another important task—to write Hideyo's name large on the pages of the newspaper in India ink and our address in the corner. Ko made a pot of paste with flour and water.

We had to break the ice in the stream next morning to wash. Ko put pieces of ice in the mess kits and built a fire to melt it. She poured hot water into a borrowed wash pan, and we took it upstairs and washed. What was left in the mess kits we drank, to warm ourselves.

Going to the toilet, in the outhouse, was a cold business too. I let Ko go first because she left a little body heat and warm footprints where I squatted.

Then we went to Maizuru, Ko carrying the little items we had made and I the paste and Hideyo's name papers. Hideyo's name was not on record at the refugee center as having landed, so we pasted the name papers on the bulletin board, the walls of the port, and just everywhere. Every inch of space was filled with other names and messages.

All that Saturday we stayed in the vicinity of the port to sell our items. Some housewives with small children were delighted to buy the toys and clothes. Others went through them, then changed their minds, and our hearts sank. At some houses well-dressed, well-made-up housewives looked us over and slammed the door. But we kept on trying houses all day.

Finally we had sold everything. Ko bought two hot sweet potatoes from a pushcart man and we sat on a concrete wall by the waterfront, swinging our legs, letting the December wind blow our inch-and-a-half-long hair, and ate the potatoes. The sun sank slowly, leaving a gorgeous crimson display on the water. As it tucked the earth to rest, we held hands and headed for home.

Finally New Year's Eve day arrived. Ko was not feeling well and she overslept. She jumped from the bed mumbling that she would be late for class, and told me to come straight home from school and build the fire because she had something to do at the University.

"Why do you have to do it on New Year's Eve day?" I complained. "I'm afraid to build the fire."

"Do it! It's about time you learned to do things." She grabbed her books and blanket. "Don't forget to lock the door."

I had ill feeling toward Ko. Because of that idea of hers she had not been there when Mother died, and how Mother had wanted to see her. Since Mother died she had become bossier than ever, and now she was telling me to come home fast and build a fire for supper. We had nothing to eat in the apple box cabinet, nothing to make a meal of. Ko had been handling all the money so I had no money to buy groceries. I was not about to spend my little earnings beneath Mother's urn. That was for my shoes. No, I would not come right home from school. I would sell some more items and earn some more money.

I had learned to take the girls' abuse, but remembering the way Ko had left the warehouse and my talking back made me terribly lonely during the day, especially when a girl asked me, "How long are you coming to school with rags on?" I longed for Father and Mother, and wished Father would come home safely to embrace me in his wide arms.

As I gathered papers in the furnace room I was sniffing and wiping away tears and wondering when I could lead a normal life with Father and Hideyo. How I envied the girls who lived with their parents and sisters and brothers. I could almost see and hear their happy laughter at mealtime.

Mr. Naido came and emptied cans into a huge box. When he saw me he took out his billfold and handed me five yen, saying I had done well collecting cans and should keep it up. He would take my cans anytime.

Then he said, without much stuttering, "Why tears?"

"I was thinking of my father and brother," I said slowly. "I hope they are not dead." I sniffed some more.

"They will return. I know they will," said Mr. Naido, and wished me Happy New Year.

Because it was New Year's Eve day I had a feeling that many people would be going to a shrine or to the central part of the city. Instead of going from house to house I decided to stand on the street among the small pushcart shops. Perhaps people going home from work would stop and buy what I displayed.

I chose the Kitano shrine, popular for the pushcart shops and always busy at rush hours. Many people were buying things from the pushcarts, and I looked for a good busy spot to display my wares.

Suddenly I saw Ko. She sat on the cold ground polishing a man's shoes. I froze. I realized then that with this *idea* she had been feeding me. And now I was sure she wanted to get some traditional foods, perhaps fluffy rice cakes, to welcome the brand-new year.

Oh, Honorable Sister! I swallowed lumps.

Ko finished polishing the man's shoes. He handed her money and she put it in her pocket. The man, his shoes shiny as a new coin, passed by me. Ko put on her soldier's hat, caped herself with her blanket, and called, "Shoe shine! Shoe shine!"

I turned and hurried homeward, Ko's clear shoeshine call sounding in my good ear all the way. I spent my shoe money and the five yen I had earned from selling cans to Mr. Naido to buy something good to eat for my honorable sister and me, something for our New Year's Eve feast.

Snow was falling when I got home from the general store. I had bought two cups of rice, a fish, narrow strips of seaweed, an orange, a tiny bag of green tea, and a small, cheaply made teapot. I wanted to pour green tea for Ko at our New Year's Eve feast.

First I had to build a fire. Leaving my small rucksack with all the things I had bought by the stairway, I went to the back side of the warehouse, beneath the eaves, where Ko had made a small *hibachi* with stones. I crumpled some newspapers and added wood scraps that Ko had gathered the night before to dry out. When the pieces caught fire I added thick blocks and fanned with a piece of cardboard as Ko always did. But the fire died, leaving nothing but smoke. I repeated the procedure, using more paper and more scraps, and when it was good and red I put on the blocks that had not burned. I fanned and kept on fanning until the blocks began to burn.

I set the mess kit on the fire. It had been filled with water before I left for school, but now the water was ice. While it melted I went to the outside tap for drinking water, but the tap was frozen. So I rushed to the stream, cracked the frozen water with my heels, and put all the ice chips into the bucket, to wash and cook the rice.

The water in the mess kit was boiling vigorously when Ko appeared, covered with snow. "It's very cold and windy!" she said. She shook the snow from her blanket and soldier's hat.

"Honorable Sister, welcome home," I said. "Your hot water is ready."

"I knew you could do it," said Ko.

"I think we need another hibachi to cook our supper," I said.

"Why?"

"One to cook rice, one to roast the fish."

"Who said we were going to roast a fish?" asked Ko.

"I did. I bought a fish."

"Where did you get the money?"

"Mr. Naido paid me for the cans and I used my shoe money."

"Oh! You dummy!" exclaimed Ko, but she did not sound angry. "I had money. See?" She pulled out a few yen from an inside pocket, and on my mental screen I saw her shining shoes and calling to get more customers.

"It's New Year's Eve. I will be twelve! You will be seventeen!" I said. "We must celebrate." In Japan everyone gains a year not on the date of his birth but at the New Year.

Ko set the bucket on the hot fire for the rice and drank some of the hot water in the bowl to warm herself, and while she did that I managed to take the tea bag and teapot from my rucksack and hide them in my overcoat pocket.

We did need another hibachi. We gathered stones, some frozen to the ground, and Ko built a fire. She washed the rice, saving the white rice water, and told me to wash the fish in it, but leave the head and insides as they were. Then she found a long stick, sharpened and smoothed it to make a skewer, and I roasted the fish, squatting next to Ko as she cooked the rice and made miso soup with seaweed.

It was a humble New Year's Eve meal that we ate in our home, but both of us were overwhelmed by it. We wondered what Father and Hideyo were eating that night, and how they were keeping themselves warm. We knew the severe winter in Manchuria and northern Korea.

Ko saw the orange in front of Mother's urn. I should not have bought that expensive fruit, she told me.

"I could not afford flowers for Mother on New Year's," I said. "We can eat the orange sometime."

"Go out and get your mess kit," said Ko. "The hot water will be ready for us to drink."

So I went down. I rinsed the teapot, my heart bouncing at the thought of Ko's surprised and joyful face when I made tea for her.

As I came back up Ko was setting aside the wooden rice bowls and chopsticks. And in the center of the apple-box table were fluffy red and white rice cakes, the New Year's traditional food!

"Happy New Year, Little One," said Ko, bowing slightly. "The rice cakes are for you."

"Happy New Year, Honorable Sister." I bowed to her deeply, for all her efforts and all her concern for me. I put the rice bowls back on the table. I brought out the still-wet teapot from one pocket and the tea bag from the other. "Green tea is for you," I said, and poured the tea into her bowl.

Suddenly Ko was crying. "Don't you dare spend any more of your shoe money!" she scolded, sniffing back the tears. "We can live without tea."

But she received her wooden rice bowl of green tea reverently in both hands, sipped it slowly, and let the tears roll down her face. "Ah, fine tea. I never expected this. Thank you, Little One!"

Chapter 10

During the ten-day New Year's vacation Ko finished my overcoat made from the soldiers' uniforms. Its lining was nothing but patches, but to me it was the most gorgeous thing I had ever owned. I was very happy. I wore my red overcoat now as a jacket in the house.

Even when it snowed heavily on Saturday we went to Maizuru and stayed there all day, replacing Hideyo's name papers and selling our items. Snow went into my slapping shoes and I lost feeling in my toes.

When school began again we learned that tuition would go up fifteen yen a month. Mother had paid up to April, so I owed the school forty-five yen. How could I earn all that? With snow on the ground I couldn't see any cans lying about. Maybe if I worked hard helping Ko make some of the little things, and sold them, I could earn fifteen yen a month.

When I told Ko about the increase in tuition she said this was an absolute necessity and the time had come to use Mother's wrapping cloth money. She took out a hundred yen, changed it into smaller bills at the bank, and gave me what I needed. I asked if her university tuition had gone up. It would go up in April, she said, and she would take a break from school and work somewhere until I left school. But until April she was going to enjoy every moment of her school days.

"Don't your classmates abuse you at all?" I asked.

"They did at first," Ko said, "but they learned that I can sew a white silk-lined kimono with colored thread and it doesn't show. They were so amazed they stopped abusing me."

"Why did you use colored thread on white silk?"

"Someone hid my white thread just before the testing began." Even with the shoe shining her hands always remained smooth.

No matter how hard I tried to sell Ko's little items, I did not do well in January. My left shoe, like an angry wild animal's mouth, stayed open, and even though I tied it with rope it came apart as I walked. I knew Ko would get me a pair of shoes if I complained of being cold and numb, but I wanted to hang on to the little money left in the wrapping cloth.

Ko was always figuring out what she had earned by polishing shoes, what to buy for our meals, and how far the money could be stretched. I never told her I had seen her at the shrine.

"We may have to use some of Mother's money for food this winter," she said. "I hate to touch it."

I suggested we look in the garbage bins behind the hotel.

"I won't let you do that anymore," she told me. "We're fortunate. We have a place to live, free, and a place to cook what little we buy."

Deep inside I wondered how we were going to manage until spring. Everyone was wearing boots now and surely Ko did not have many customers.

All I can do, I thought, is spend long hours after school selling Ko's handcrafts on the street or from door to door.

One morning I decided to walk to school along the tracks, the shortest way. I passed five stations, each with a bench to sit on, and I was relieved that no schoolgirls sat waiting for the streetcar. At the sixth station, scattered newspapers flapped in the January wind. I picked some up. They would make fuel for

Ko and me to warm our hands, even if there was nothing to eat.

I enjoyed discovering something we could use. Then, as I smoothed out the newspapers on the bench, I saw a headline—"Essay Contest."

I sat on the bench to read it, and I checked how old the paper was. It was the *Asahi,* the morning paper, of that day! I became more interested, and read it as I walked toward the school.

> Group 1 University
> Group 2 Boys' and Girls' Schools
> Group 3 Elementary Schools
> TITLE: OPEN
> NO MORE THAN 50 PAGES OF
> MANUSCRIPT PAPER
> PRIZES:
> FIRST PLACE ¥10,000
> SECOND PLACE ¥5,000
> THIRD PLACE ¥1,000
> CLOSING DAY: END OF FEBRUARY

A streetcar was coming, and I stepped aside and kept on reading. My thoughts were filled with prize money. If I could win at least third prize Ko and I could buy food for a couple of weeks.

The streetcar passed with a roar, leaving sparkles between wheels and rails. A girl yelled from a broken window, "Rag Doll!" I bit my lip, feeling anger I could not control and wanting to smack that girl, whoever she was. I stamped the ties and pretended I was stamping on her.

Going home I walked the tracks again, but instead of stamping I was thinking about what I could write to win the prize. Money! For food, hot food in our stomachs.

Day after day I walked the tracks and day after day I created sentences. They wanted fifty pages of manuscript paper, and each manuscript sheet had four hundred one-centimeter blocks. So I must fill out twenty thousand letters in those blocks.

I had no money to buy manuscript paper, so I made my own by drawing four hundred blocks lightly on the back of papers from the trash. I carefully filled each block. On the last day of the month I did not go to school but walked all the way to Sanjo Street, looking for the Asahi Newspaper Company, Kyoto Division. I tossed my manuscript into the large box at the entrance because I did not have money to mail it.

The paper had said the winners would be announced in two weeks; so when that time came I went to the school library. Could I, could I have won? But the librarian said the principal was reading the morning paper. I was deeply disappointed. Yet I could not go to the principal's office to ask to see the paper, so I had to wait until the next day.

Next morning, walking to school, I was very nervous. I wanted so much to win.

Our classroom was noisier than usual. I took my seat and suddenly all was quiet. The entire class was looking at me. I did not understand it, but I took out my English reader. English was my favorite subject and our teacher, Mr. Yoshida, always asked me to read a whole chapter. I thought he would do so today and I did not want to stumble.

A girl came and tossed a newspaper on top of my English book. What manners, I thought. I gave one glance at the paper, then I looked again. Then I picked it up and read it.

"From Group 2, Sagano Girls' School Student Sweeps Field," said the headline. There was my name, printed large and clear, with the title of my essay, "Understanding."

In my heart I laughed and laughed with joy. I made fists, for I could not shout there. Then I shed tears, thinking of how happy Ko would be and how we could both go to the grocery store for rice, miso, even tofu! We would have a feast! This was the second time I had won an essay contest. When I was in first grade in Korea I wrote a story, "Canary Bird," that was published in a newspaper. I began reading my own essay.

In it I had criticized the Sagano Girls' School students for snobbish behavior, but this made little difference in the way my classmates treated me. Perhaps they were not so mean and sarcastic in the days that followed, but they were very cold. I was sure they had not liked my essay. Not a single teacher mentioned the prize. Obviously the school was not pleased.

The newspaper gave a banquet for the contest winners. Ko took tucks in her school uniform for me to wear, but I had to be accompanied by a guardian. In Japan all guardians must be parents or must be male even if the male is a baby brother. I had no one, but I desperately wanted to go to the banquet.

Then I thought of Mr. Naido, and he was delighted. Of course he would go with me. No one asked who he was. I would have said he was my uncle. He did not even stutter very much.

I had not eaten such food, or so much food, for months. I slipped half into the newspaper I had brought, for Ko.

And I received my ten thousand yen. But I did not buy shoes even though Ko wanted me to. That prize money would feed us for many weeks and we would not have to use more of the money in the wrapping cloth. The wrapping cloth money was our security.

A week later I was called to the office by the principal. I had been afraid that sooner or later I would be sent for and suspended because of my essay, but I had that prize money, the difference between eating and starving for Ko and me. I had decided I could take suspension.

"Sit down, Miss Kawashima," ordered the bald-headed principal. I sat. "Do you know a man by the name of Matsumura?"

I thought for a moment. "I knew a Corporal Matsumura in Korea."

The principal showed me a square white envelope. "This letter came addressed to you in care of the school. I opened it."

The letter couldn't have come from the Corporal. He belonged to my past. He didn't know where I was. My heart began to pound. Then I suddenly remembered that Father had forbidden his children to open each other's mail, and first things first.

"Sir," I said, "you shouldn't have done that."

"I feel responsible for you. You are a very young maiden."

Stubbornness forced me on. "You should have given it to me first. I would have shown it to you, sir."

He handed me the envelope without replying, and I took out the letter. A self-addressed postcard was enclosed and the letter was on the paper of Kyoto's Sanjo Hotel. I read:

To Miss Kawashima Yoko,

I am not sure I am writing to the right young lady. Your name character, Yoko, struck me after I read your essay in the newspaper. The only Yoko I know using this character lived in Nanam, Korea, a little girl who came to see me when I was in the hospital. If you are the same person please reply. I enclose a postcard.

Sincerely,
Mr. Matsumura

Halfway through his letter I began shedding tears, and they rolled down both cheeks to my chin and dropped on the letter paper. Ah! Corporal Matsumura! He had lived through the dangerous war. He must have crawled under the showers of bombs and fire. I looked at the principal, sobbing, and said brokenly, "Sir, Mr. Matsumura is a friend of our family."

"Then the letter is yours."

I could not wait for school to end that day. I ran and skipped along the rail ties and excitedly showed the letter to Ko. She read it over and over, not able to believe, and she shed tears of gladness too, to hear from him and know he had been spared.

"What is he doing in this city?" she wondered.

In very small characters I wrote on the postcard that I was the one he was looking for, and that I was studying hard even though we had almost starved, and that Mother had died at the train station in November. We were like two orphans, I told him, for we were separated from Father and Hideyo. I added, "My thoughts often go back to the happy days, but someday I trust good fortune will come my way again."

I walked to the small post office next to the general store and mailed it right away, hoping he would receive it before he left the city.

How I wanted to see the Corporal! How I wanted to go to the Sanjo Hotel. But such a visit was strictly prohibited by our customs; no maiden should ever visit a man, especially in a hotel. For Ko and me it was even worse, for we had no guardian. I had not told the principal that Mother had been dead for three and a half months, for the school did not accept students without an established guardian.

As we sipped miso soup I told Ko I wished she were married. Her husband would be my guardian and he would take me to see the Corporal.

"At least he is alive and well," Ko reminded me. "We will meet him someday."

I even thought of calling the hotel, but I felt it was awkward.

Such a mean world! "Nothing goes right for me!" I complained. "It's been like *hell!*"

"Let's hope there will never be war again as long as we live," said Ko.

Strong north winds shook the warehouse that night and drafts came in from everywhere. We were cold. Ko doubled our mattress, using the extra futon. She put all the covers on us and we snuggled together for warmth.

It was two days after I had mailed the postcard, and our class was doing a silkworm experiment in the laboratory during the last period, when Mr. Naido came in and spoke to Mr. Iwai, the biology teacher.

"Miss Kawashima," called the teacher, "report to the principal's office."

Why did the principal want me again? The only thing I had done wrong was that I had not told him about Mother. I was going to tell him when my tuition ran out and I could not go to school anymore. Or was my appearance so bad that he didn't want me in the school? Or could it be, even now, that essay?

My heart beat loudly as I stood at the office door. I combed through my two-inch-long hair with my fingers. I opened the door quietly and bowed to the principal.

"Here she is!" he said.

A man wearing a dark blue pinstripe suit turned. "Oh!" I exclaimed. That scarred face . . . and familiar smile! "Oh, Corporal Ma—" I ran toward him and threw myself into his arms and sobbed. How safe I felt in his arms.

The Corporal held me with one arm, stroking my porcupine hair, his tears falling on my head.

"Little One, Little One!" he said. "I had to see you before I left the city. When does your sister get home?"

"About six." I was still crying.

"Take me to your place. We have much to talk about."

I returned to the laboratory, gathered my belongings, and rushed back. The principal and Corporal Matsumura were talking in low voices, and I sat and waited. I had sat on this chair when Mother and I first came to the school, I remembered.

How joyous it was to ride the streetcar with the Corporal all the way to our warehouse. I led him upstairs. There was no cushion to welcome my important guest so I folded my blanket four times and asked him to sit on it.

The Corporal met with Mother's urn. He bowed deeply, his eyes closed. Then I heard Ko and rushed downstairs to take her hand and bring her up quickly to meet our honorable guest.

Ko tried hard not to show tears when she met the Corporal, but she pulled out her handkerchief, barely able to say, "Welcome!"

He was in the city on business. As we ate our humble supper and after we had told our story, he told us that he had left Nanam the day after we fled. He was assigned to the Niigata Army Hospital in the homeland, but as his ship crossed the Sea of Japan it was attacked by American bombers. He had floated, holding on to a log, for four days until he was rescued by a Japanese fishing boat. Then the atomic bombs had been dropped, the war had ended, and he had returned to his hometown, Morioka, a castle town where long ago Lord Taira had lived and governed the district. The Corporal had taken over his father's silk thread and textile business, which had been passed down from ancestors who had woven materials for the lord of the castle and his family.

"Oh, that was why you felt my costume at the hospital!" I exclaimed.

"Right," he said. "I could feel the quality of the materials."

His marriage had been arranged upon his return to his hometown, and now he and his wife were expecting a baby. He gazed at me and he said lovingly, "If it is a girl I shall name her Yoko."

"By the way," he continued, "I kept your calligraphy, *Bu Un Cho Kyu,* in my uniform pocket. It was soaked, but I framed it and it hangs in my office. It has brought me good luck."

Corporal Matsumura wanted to buy me a pair of shoes but the stores were already closed. He also wanted to help us with our daily expenses, but we told him we had enough money for now. He gave us his address and made us promise to wire him collect when we did need something—anything. We would hear from him soon, he said.

He was taking the midnight express, and Ko and I went to the station to see him off. Mother had left me at this station, and now the Corporal was leaving too. Loneliness attacked me and once more sobs wracked my body.

"Here," said the Corporal, taking off his wristwatch. "I noticed you have no clock. Keep this and give it to your brother as a welcome. No more tears, Little One. Keep up your good work."

A station bell's sound burst in the air, warning that the train was leaving. The Corporal jumped on and took his seat. He waved at us through the window, and Ko and I bowed to him deeply for his friendship. I held his wristwatch tightly.

The train began moving. He waved to us again. I put the watch to my good ear and it was ticking and warm. I read his lips. "We'll keep in touch." The train increased speed. Ko and I watched until we could no longer see the red taillight.

Chapter 11

In a small farmhouse near the thirty-eighth parallel lived Mr. and Mrs. Kim and their boys, Hee Cho, sixteen, and Hee Wang, fourteen. They were having supper when there was a loud thud outside the kitchen door.

"Probably the wind," said Mr. Kim, eating his fluffy rice with *kimch'i,* the hot Korean pickle. "The snow has changed to a blizzard."

"Hee Cho, go check," said Mrs. Kim.

The thin wooden door was usually easy to slide open with a toe, but this time Hee Cho could not move it. The door was off the track, and he tried to put it back. "Something is pushing the door," he called.

"Maybe the wild boar again." Mr. Kim got up, went into the earthen-floor kitchen, and picked up a large broadax. Hee Wang came with a rope and Mrs. Kim brought a lantern. Mr. Kim gave his elder son the broadax while he worked on the door.

He could not get it back on the track. Mr. Kim thought the wild boar would be pacing around the barn, not pushing against their door. Finally he lifted the door and removed it completely from the track. Wind and snow blew in, and Hideyo lay there, unconscious.

Mr. Kim touched his garments. "Frozen." They carried Hideyo in and put the door back on the track while the wind howled and the snow blew in.

The boys brought straw and mats from the barn and made a bed on the dirt floor. Mr. Kim removed the rucksack and Mrs. Kim tore off the thin, torn

Korean garments. A Japanese student's uniform appeared.

"Is he a Japanese boy, Father?" asked Hee Wang.

"The way he carried his rucksack and the cherry flower emblem on the buttons of the uniform show he is Japanese," his father told him.

They took off leg wrappers, shoes, and wet socks. Hideyo wore four pairs of socks, half-frozen, and all the shirts he owned. Mrs. Kim wiped his body and massaged his chest.

"Look what I found," exclaimed Hee Wang. "A belly wrapper, with a notebook in it."

The notebook was a Japanese savings book. "What's his name, son?" asked Mr. Kim. Both of his boys could read the characters for "Kawashima." They hid the savings book and the contents of the rucksack, in case the Communist Army came to inspect the house.

Mrs. Kim put more wood in the clay firebox that heated the cooking vat and the rest of the house. While the men massaged Hideyo's legs and body, Mrs. Kim put crushed hot pepper in dry socks, put the socks on Hideyo's feet, and wrapped the feet in the little fur coat. More crushed dry pepper went onto Hideyo's chest, as the massage continued.

They put a nightshirt on him, covered him with a blanket, and tucked lots of straw over and around him. "He will be all right while we eat," Mr. Kim said.

As they ate, the farmer made his decision. "If he should die or if anyone finds out we have rescued a Japanese boy, we will be betrayed for prize money and executed. Listen, everyone. The boy is going to be my nephew. His parents were killed by Japanese and he has come to live with us. Do you understand? This way we are not in danger."

They ate quickly and then Mrs. Kim crushed garlic,

added warm water, and tried to feed Hideyo as Mr. Kim forced open his mouth. His throat contracted—he swallowed. His feet were warming a little but his hands were ice-cold. Crushed pepper went into mittens for his hands.

Long after their sons had gone to bed Mr. and Mrs. Kim massaged Hideyo's body, kept water boiling for steam, and fed him garlic water with crushed hot peppers in it. Mr. Kim was feeding logs into the fire when his wife called out, "*Aboji* (Daddy)! He turned and groaned!" Mr. Kim rushed back and patted Hideyo's cheeks.

Honorable Brother returned to life, so tired that he could not move. He did not know where he was or who these people were. And where were his things? He was even fearful of being poisoned when the woman held a spoon to his lips. She tasted the pepper and garlic water to show him it was safe, and the hot mixture felt good to his stomach.

He told them who he was and where he had come from, and Hee Cho, when he came home from school, told him, "You are going to be our cousin."

Of course Hideyo wanted to be on his way to Seoul, but he was in no condition to travel. Besides, Mr. Kim told him, everyone trying to escape to the south had been killed by the Communist Army. "Now you are our relative," the farmer said. "Stay with us until you regain your health. You will be at home here."

As soon as he was able to get up, Hideyo helped the family, weaving straw, repairing the barn. Often he went to town with Mr. Kim to sell the straw mats they made. After supper he would fetch two wooden buckets of water on a pole across his shoulders, to fill a large tub in the kitchen, so Mrs. Kim would not have to walk on the icy path. He got up early to build a fire and heat water.

He helped Hee Wang with arithmetic and discussed politics with Hee Cho in the Korean language. He learned a political vocabulary.

Spring came. Hideyo helped remove the protective straw from the apple trees, and as the fragrance of apple blossoms filled the air and bees danced from blossom to blossom, his thoughts drifted to his birthplace, Aomori, in Japan, where lots of apples were grown. Then the images of his parents revived in his heart, for they too were born in apple blossom country. Homesickness for his parents and sisters overwhelmed him, and one evening as they ate supper he told the Kim family he must leave.

"Stay. Become our boy," said Mr. Kim.

"Please stay!" begged Hee Cho and Hee Wang.

Mrs. Kim was in tears.

But he must go, Hideyo said. As soon as the spring work was finished and when the moon was dark, so that he would not be spotted.

When the last supper with the generous Korean family was finished, he gathered his few belongings. His student's uniform, underwear, pants, and socks were washed and folded by Mrs. Kim. Hideyo put the fur coat in the bottom of the rucksack, then the family album and savings book, then his clothes.

Mrs. Kim packed large rice balls in a bamboo box and Mr. Kim handed Hideyo a little money. Hideyo tried to refuse the money, for Mr. Kim was a poor farmer who had to give almost all his earnings to the government, but Mr. Kim insisted that he carry some Korean money.

He wanted to tell Mrs. Kim many things to express his gratitude, but the tears came and his chest tightened. Mrs. Kim held his hands and cried, "*Aigo!*" an expression of sadness. He shook hands with Mr. Kim, and the hand, rough from years of hard work in the fields, seemed gentle and soft. Mr. Kim, in tears, bit his chapped lips and nodded his wrinkled face, as if to say, "Don't say anything. I understand."

Then, because a rucksack would give away the fact that he was Japanese, Mrs. Kim put the rucksack in a burlap bag tied with a long rope and told him to carry it around his hips like a Korean.

Hee Cho went with Hideyo as far as the river. Imjŏn, the fourth-largest river in Korea, crosses the thirty-eighth parallel. American soldiers controlled southern Korea, and Hideyo knew he would be safer once he crossed this boundary. The river was four miles from the Kims' house. As they left the house the sun was about to set. Hideyo kept looking back, waving to Mr. and Mrs. Kim and Hee Wang. Just before they vanished into the deep forest he waved a towel three times for a final farewell. At their doorway the Kims waved back.

The river was well guarded by the Communists. From a watchtower nearby, a searchlight swept over the area, throwing its strong beam on the river surface. Hideyo untied his burlap bag and took off all his clothes, even his rubber-soled tabi. He shoved them all into the bag, put the bag on his head, and fastened it to him with the rope. That way, if the bag fell off his head it would still be tied to him.

He cast his eyes onto the dark, wide river and wondered if he could swim across. The thought flashed through his mind that if he was spotted and killed, this running water would be crimsoned by his blood.

The boys looked at each other. They shook hands.

Hee Cho whispered, "*Chosim haesŏ kaseyo* (Go carefully)."

"*Komapsŭmnida* (Thank you)," whispered Hideyo.

"*Chaphi jianko kaseyo* (Travel so that you do not get caught)."

"*ŭnhe rŭl ichi an gesŭmnida* (I will not forget your kindness)."

"*Chigŭm kaseyo* (Go now)!"

When the searchlight had passed over them, Hideyo slipped into the river. It was much colder than he had expected and the current was very strong. He swam. Each time a light came toward him he dove under, so that only his bag showed, half submerged and looking, he hoped, like a floating log. Again and again he had to dive.

Gunfire burst in the air, echoing in a thousand directions. Hideyo did not know whether it was aimed at him, at some other escapees, or at wild animals. The light swept over him again and he submerged deeper. He could see the shore not far from him, but the current kept pushing him downstream and so many submergings slowed him.

Again gunfire. A bullet hit the bag on Hideyo's head and dropped to the surface. He could hear the bullets piercing the waters all around him. He dove deeper and let the current carry him. Then he swam again. When he finally reached the south side he lay as dead when the light shone his way, then crawled toward the bushes, exhausted.

He had escaped across the dangerous thirty-eighth parallel. He took a deep breath of freedom. He thanked God for the Kim family and hoped that they would see in a dream that he had made it to the other side.

His Korean clothes, protected by the fur coat, blanket, and the family album, were only damp, and he put them on. He had been carried so far by the current that he did not know his direction, so he spread his wet blanket and slept.

The sky was bright when he woke. He ate one rice ball filled with kimch'i, the Korean pickle that he liked so much. As he ate the hot, garlicky pickle he remembered reaching the Kims' house in the blizzard, and being returned to consciousness with Mrs. Kim there.

He had been saved, one step from death, and now he was no longer afraid of getting caught or being shot. He walked joyfully, eagerly searching through the bushes to locate the road. At a farmhouse he asked directions to Seoul and took fast steps toward the city. He still carried that burlap bag around his hips, and for some reason he did not want to carry a rucksack, as a Japanese boy should. Perhaps he wanted to follow the Korean custom as a sign of love for Mrs. Kim. He walked about forty miles.

In Seoul he went straight to the railroad station, where Mother's note had said she and her daughters would be waiting. But he did not see his loved ones. He asked station workers, but so many Japanese women had come by with their children that they could not help him.

For seven nights he slept in a corner of the station, searching for his family during the days. He began to wonder if they had been killed. Then he went to the American Red Cross, which was now helping Japanese and Korean escapees. The Kawashima name was not listed in the register of refugees.

Maybe they had been lucky enough to get back to Japan. He asked for a certificate as a refugee, so that he could get on the train to Pusan and then on the boat to Japan.

For the first time in eight months, since he had left Nanam, he was riding. It was a flatcar on a freight train, so filled with escapees that there was little space for him to sit. But he was just so glad that he did not have to walk. As the train began to move he gazed absently at the station poles, not knowing that on them were messages carved by his sisters: "Hideyo, we wait at Pusan."

At Pusan harbor the boats periodically made their runs to Japan with refugees. Hideyo landed at Maizuru. And discovered his name written on a piece of newspaper with his sisters' address.

He shouted for joy. "Little One's writing!"

Though it was a harsh winter for Ko and me, the reunion with Corporal Matsumura made our lives more bearable. He and Mrs. Matsumura often sent us packages containing leftover materials, threads, dried fish, pickles, and rice. The Corporal even took orders from his clients for kimono garments and asked Ko to make them. Though he lived many miles away, each time a package or letter came we felt he was near. He never failed to enclose stamps and asked us to tell him all our doings and about our progress in learning.

One day he wrote to say he had put Father's and Hideyo's names on the nationwide broadcasting station called "Search for Persons." He told us to listen at ten a.m. weekends, if we were home, and at six p.m. weekdays.

We asked Mr. Masuda for permission to listen at six p.m. Holding hands, we stood in front of the radio. I even looked up at the radio on its shelf as if to listen to the Corporal speaking to me. At six the announcer opened the program. Holding hands more tightly, we waited for Father's and Hideyo's names to come out. Sure enough: "If anyone has seen Kawashima Yoshio or his son Hideyo, or has information about them, contact Mr. Matsumura at his silk textile company, Morioka, Japan."

We continued to make gift items and sell them after school, and every Saturday we made the trip to Maizuru with fresh name papers. In our bits of free time Ko taught me how to make a blouse and skirt from the leftover materials the Corporal sent. Life was a little easier. All I needed now was Father and Hideyo.

What was taking them so long? It was April, cherry blossoms were in full bloom, birds were singing their love songs in the cedar forest at the Myoshinji temple. Soon there would be a nest and family. Were Father and Hideyo dead? If I knew they were dead I would give up hope, but not knowing frustrated me.

The school term ended and I made straight A's. But I knew I would not be going to school anymore, for the tuition money had run out. I rushed to the furnace room to show my report sheet to Mr. Naido.

"You made it!" Smiling, he pulled three yen from his billfold for cans he had sold and handed me two extra yen, congratulating me. "K-keep it up!" He patted my back.

He had been such a sincere friend to me, and he had no one else to talk to in the school. I could not tell him I was quitting.

Miss Asada announced that the class was going to the flower viewing that afternoon, and everyone was excited. They were all stowing belongings in bags for vacation. I thought, What's such a big deal about going to see cherry blossoms? I had no space in my heart for such frolicking. I had more important things to do.

And I had a new worry besides the struggle to live— my eyes. I could not see the teacher's writing on the blackboard. I also had a hard time hearing the soft-spoken teachers.

I asked permission to be excused from going to the

flower viewing, using as an excuse Ko's university style show, which I said I wanted to see. But I did not go to the style show, I went from door to door displaying our wares. Each time I made a sale I put the money in the small bag Ko had made, and put it in my inside trousers pocket.

I rushed home in time to fix supper for Ko. With better weather she stayed on the street to polish shoes and hurried home just before six so we could listen to the radio. Then she started supper. But tonight I wanted to have something good for us. Maybe a fish. I had money, from the cans and sales and Mr. Naido's gift.

At the general store I bought a fish and with my one remaining yen I bought two tea bags. With this tea I could celebrate with Honorable Sister my good report sheet.

At the stream I scaled the fish. Soft green dandelion leaves were shooting up from the soil, and I left the fish wrapped in a large bamboo leaf and went back with a bucket and peeling knife.

I had gotten much more skillful in building a fire in the small stone-ringed fireplace. I put the bucket of water on the fire with the dandelions in it, but the greens shrank so much that I fished them out and went back with the bucket for more.

As I turned to go back to the fireplace, through the glass doors of the factory I saw a man walking by. He was carrying a burlap bag on his hips in Korean fashion, and I remembered how Mr. and Mrs. Lee used to carry their belongings that way when they were not carrying things on their heads. For a while I dreamed of happy bygone days.

Again I went back for dandelions, and again as I returned the young man passed, walking slowly toward the general store.

Perhaps he is a Korean who is not familiar with this area, I thought. Maybe he cannot speak Japanese and can't find what he is looking for. Perhaps I can help him. But first I had to find a skewer for the fish and lay it across the stones and squeeze greens.

Then I stepped out to the front of the warehouse. He had turned and was coming back. Beyond the warehouse were only open fields, no house or person for him to find. He stood, then walked toward me. "Good evening," he called in perfect Japanese. I waited for him to come nearer, so I could see and hear him clearly.

"Oh! Little One! Little One!" He was rushing toward me.

I stood there, half in shock, and then I cried out and threw myself into his arms. "Welcome home, Honorable Brother!"

That night, as dark enveloped our humble sleeping place, I made three beds. One for Hideyo, to rest well. As I lay in mine I saw the stars shining like petals of white chrysanthemums. For the first time since I had left Nanam I felt their loveliness. And each star that sparkled was like great fireworks in the enormous sky for the gladness of our reunion.

Related Readings

CONTENTS

Refugee Mother and Child

by Chinua Achebe

As Yoko's family flees from Korea, she experiences the best and the worst of humanity—miracles of love amid the horrors of war. As you read, think about the bond described in this poem. What relationships in Yoko's memoir does the poem call to mind?

No Madonna and Child could touch
that picture of a mother's tenderness
for a son she soon would have to forget.

The air was heavy with odours
5   of diarrhoea of unwashed children
with washed-out ribs and dried-up
bottoms struggling in laboured
steps behind blown empty bellies. Most
mothers there had long ceased
10   to care but not this one; she held
a ghost smile between her teeth
and in her eyes the ghost of a mother's
pride as she combed the rust-coloured
hair left on his skull and then—
15   singing in her eyes—began carefully
to part it . . . In another life this
must have been a little daily
act of no consequence before his
breakfast and school; now she
20   did it like putting flowers
on a tiny grave.

Old Man at the Bridge

by Ernest Hemingway

Yoko and her family become part of a throng of refugees who live from moment to moment, shadowed by the fear of capture or death. The following story, which is set during the Spanish Civil War of the 1930s, is also about a refugee. How would you compare the old man with the refugees whom Yoko encounters?

An old man with steel rimmed spectacles and very dusty clothes sat by the side of the road. There was a pontoon bridge across the river and carts, trucks, and men, women and children were crossing it. The mule-drawn carts staggered up the steep bank from the bridge with soldiers helping push against the spokes of the wheels. The trucks ground up and away heading out of it all and the peasants plodded along in the ankle deep dust. But the old man sat there without moving. He was too tired to go any farther.

It was my business to cross the bridge, explore the bridgehead beyond and find out to what point the enemy had advanced. I did this and returned over the bridge. There were not so many carts now and very few people on foot, but the old man was still there.

"Where do you come from?" I asked him.

"From San Carlos," he said, and smiled.

That was his native town and so it gave him pleasure to mention it and he smiled.

"I was taking care of animals," he explained.

"Oh," I said, not quite understanding.

"Yes," he said, "I stayed, you see, taking care of animals. I was the last one to leave the town of San Carlos."

He did not look like a shepherd nor a herdsman and I looked at his black dusty clothes and his gray dusty face and his steel rimmed spectacles and said, "What animals were they?"

"Various animals," he said, and shook his head. "I had to leave them."

I was watching the bridge and the African looking country of the Ebro Delta and wondering how long now it would be before we would see the enemy, and listening all the while for the first noises that would signal that ever mysterious event called contact, and the old man still sat there.

"What animals were they?" I asked.

"There were three animals altogether," he explained. "There were two goats and a cat and then there were four pairs of pigeons."

"And you had to leave them?" I asked.

"Yes. Because of the artillery. The captain told me to go because of the artillery."

"And you have no family?" I asked, watching the far end of the bridge where a few last carts were hurrying down the slope of the bank.

"No," he said, "only the animals I stated. The cat, of course, will be all right. A cat can look out for itself, but I cannot think what will become of the others."

"What politics have you?" I asked.

"I am without politics," he said. "I am seventy-six years old. I have come twelve kilometers now and I think now I can go no further."

"This is not a good place to stop," I said. "If you

can make it, there are trucks up the road where it forks for Tortosa."

"I will wait a while," he said, "and then I will go. Where do the trucks go?"

"Towards Barcelona," I told him.

"I know no one in that direction," he said, "but thank you very much. Thank you again very much."

He looked at me very blankly and tiredly, then said, having to share his worry with some one, "The cat will be all right, I am sure. There is no need to be unquiet about the cat. But the others. Now what do you think about the others?"

"Why they'll probably come through it all right."

"You think so?"

"Why not?" I said, watching the far bank where now there were no carts.

"But what will they do under the artillery when I was told to leave because of the artillery?"

"Did you leave the dove cage unlocked?" I asked.

"Yes."

"Then they'll fly."

"Yes, certainly they'll fly. But the others. It's better not to think about the others," he said.

"If you are rested I would go," I urged. "Get up and try to walk now."

"Thank you," he said and got to his feet, swayed from side to side and then sat down backwards in the dust.

"I was taking care of animals," he said dully, but no longer to me. "I was only taking care of animals."

There was nothing to do about him. It was Easter Sunday and the Fascists were advancing toward the Ebro. It was a gray overcast day with a low ceiling so their planes were not up. That and the fact that cats know how to look after themselves was all the good luck that old man would ever have.

from The Endless Steppe: Growing Up in Siberia

by Esther Hautzig

Former strangers such as Corporal Matsumura touch Yoko's life deeply. In the following excerpt from her memoir, Esther Hautzig describes some of her experiences with strangers as an exile in Siberia. As you read, think about connections between Esther's experiences and Yoko's.

The spring came, the rather thin spring of the Siberian steppe.

But it is impossible to have any thoughts of the thin Siberian spring without first recalling the thick mud. What with the spring rains and the thaw, the steppe became an ocean of mud and to walk through it was like walking through knee-deep molasses. If one was not lucky enough to own a pair of *sapogy,* the handsome knee-high leather boots that the well-to-do wore, if one had nothing but the same old pair of school oxfords, or even *pimy* boots, along with the energy needed to pull a foot up from the bottom of this mud, one also more often than not had to stop to hunt for the shoe left behind. Whatever one wore, the object developed a crust of mud that had to be broken off after each excursion. While I may have found some of this fun, my mother did not; her trips to and from the bakery in the mud required more energy than she had. She said that time and again,

155

exhausted, she would stand still, with both legs buried in the mud, thinking that only a derrick would be able to hoist her out.

Mud or no mud, Siberia notwithstanding, with the spring I was gay. I had a friend to whisper and gossip with; I played tag and hopscotch—which a less muddy patch in the schoolyard permitted—and along with the other girls, I watched the boys' preoccupation with their pigeons. Raising pigeons was one of their favorite pastimes, and luring the birds away from each other apparently its major objective.

Svetlana and I studied together and complemented each other: she helped me with my Russian grammar and spelling, and I helped her with ideas for themes. Although I always enjoyed school, going to school in Siberia became for me a daily trip to paradise. The return trip to the hut was not. The last day of school for me was a sad day.

As soon as school was over, we began to work on our potato crop for the coming winter.

The government had allotted individual plots of land on the outskirts of the village, and one bought tiny potatoes to sow, with the expectation that they would produce a new crop.

This was not a foregone conclusion with that unyielding earth. Very early in the morning, we would go out with shovels and sacks of potatoes to fight, cajole, and work this land. Whatever produced here would belong to us, which was worth remembering as our backs ached and our skin blistered in the sun. And what was produced, what little, *did* belong to us. There was no pilfering in the unprotected, unguarded potato plots. Considering the empty bellies, this degree of honesty was astonishing.

With summer upon us, the hut became unbearably stifling, the vermin unbearably populous, and all tempers reacted accordingly—our landladies', the little boy's, and ours. After all, ten human beings were inhabiting this wretched little oven.

Father decided to investigate the possibility of finding us new quarters.

On the north side of the village, there were some dilapidated and unoccupied huts. Unoccupied with reason: there was no heating of any kind, no floors, and no glass in the windows. But they were empty. Father went to the village housing chief and asked if we might enjoy the privilege of occupying one of these huts.

About this time, factories were beginning to be built in Rubtsovsk—among them a huge tractor factory—and with them came a large migration from European Russia of engineers, technicians of all sorts, and workers. In order to house these people, large new buildings were erected near the factories and alongside the huts. The district where they existed became known as the *novostroyka,* meaning new buildings. To me, these buildings were the ultimate in beauty and comfort. They were painted white and yellow and light green and there were floors in them and some apartments even had bathrooms, but these were only for the chiefs of the factories.

Miraculously, we were permitted to move into one of the empty huts and we were to be alone at last!

The Kaftals elected to stay on with the sisters. Inevitably, seven people who had been virtually bedfellows ended up getting on one another's nerves.

As for me, the wretched little hut became my dream house. Every day, after working in the potato patch, I went there and cleaned it as best I could. We also

from *The Endless Steppe: Growing Up in Siberia*   157

picked up manure, mixed it with clay, and either replaced some of the old square blocks in the walls or repaired others. Father got some whitewash at the construction job and we covered the walls with it. And someplace or other we found glass for the windows.

Before we could cover the floor with fresh clay, we had to dig a cold cellar. Since it would be impossible to keep the potatoes from freezing in an outdoor cellar, we dug one in the middle of our room. Father found some split logs lying around the *novostroyka* and covered the hole with them. Since the rounded logs were also still covered with bark, they gave our floor an odd look, but no matter: we had our own home and our own stove, an outdoor summer one that Father had constructed of bricks, where we could cook our own little flour cakes and our own soup without lining up to do so—and without any helpful and unhelpful, welcome and unwelcome, hints as to their preparation.

That spring Mother had learned that there was such a marvelous thing as a public bath, a *bania*, in the village, and to get there became her dearest wish. What if we did eat a little less for a week or two to save up for such a treat? Wouldn't it be heavenly to feel *clean* before we moved to our own home?

The *bania* was in a small building with two entrances, one for men and one for women. We found that Mother was not the only woman with a passion for cleanliness: the line was long; the wait would be a couple of hours at least. We waited.

There were two rooms in the *bania;* one had stone benches and faucets along the walls, the other was a steam room, a rather crude sauna where one used twigs in the Finnish fashion to clean oneself and stir up one's circulation.

We were assigned a cubbyhole for our clothes and,

since we were to use the room with the faucets, we were given a basin and a piece of pumice. We filled our basins at a faucet, sat down on a stone bench and scrubbed away. The water was *hot*. Mother was entranced. Now we were quite ready to move.

Outside the hut, there was a small piece of land that no one seemed to be using. With our potatoes, and some tomato plants and corn seed given to us by Svetlana, we would turn it into a vegetable patch.

The plans Grandmother and I were making for this garden inevitably recalled Grandfather and our garden in Vilna. As her eyes filled with tears, Grandmother tested my memory. Did I remember what Grandfather had said about the irises? and the pansies? Did I remember the lilac tree?

Yes, I remembered everything. I remembered exactly where Grandfather had said to plant each flower. I remembered the prize of fifty groshes that each week was given to the child whose flowers looked best. Yes, I remembered.

"Good!" Grandmother raised her head; she was proud of me. I had passed the test. "And you will never forget?" No, I would never forget. "Good!" Now my memory was to be honored, she seemed to say; it was to become the archive of her beloved past.

Could we plant some flowers? I wanted to know. Grandmother was a realist who lived in the future as well as the past; no, we could not, we needed every inch for growing food.

In this world of scarcity, the acquisition of the most trivial or seemingly useless object was a topic for conversation. So Svetlana told me that her father had gotten a large quantity of hospital gauze. (How and why I did not know or care to ask.) She asked me if I wanted some. I assured her I did; I would use it for curtains.

"White hospital gauze for curtains, Esther?"

"You will see," I said mysteriously.

I began to save onion peelings and asked Svetlana to do the same. In school, we had learned that onion peelings when boiled in water exuded a yellow pigment which could be used as dye. Svetlana had either forgotten this or else had no need to remember such things. She wondered what I was up to, but I told her it was a secret.

When I had gathered a big pile of onion peel, I boiled it until the water was a pot of pale yellow dye. I dunked the gauze in this, let it stay for several hours, and to my delight it worked. The gauze was now a pretty yellow. I stretched it out and dried it in the sun and then I made our curtains. There were no curtain rods to be had, so we tacked them on with little nails, and my pride in the result was very great. Everyone agreed that the curtains were very pretty and just what this hut needed.

The hut was heaven. We ate when we wanted to, slept when we wanted to, at night we would sit outside and gaze at the Siberian sky where there was always something to see; we would sit there quietly, quietly. Even Mother seemed to regain some of her old zest for life.

It was too good to be true to last.

One day the village housing chief came to our hut when I was alone and told me that the next day we were to have a tenant, whether we wanted one or not.

"Who is it going to be?" I asked.

"Vanya, the bum."

"Vanya, the bum . . . ?" I was horrified.

I had been taught never to call anyone names, but everyone called this one-legged man "Vanya the bum." He was the village beggar and people said he stole. Now this bum was going to live with us? In Vilna, there had been many beggars. Whenever I saw them, I was morbidly affected. Where did they eat? Did they ever bathe at all? And, most important, where did they go at night? Where did they sleep? Thinking about them, I used to shudder.

Now one was going to live with us.

When I gave the news to my parents, they were no less stunned than I was.

"Vanya, the bum . . . ?" Father asked.

I assured him that I had heard correctly.

Mother coughed. A signal to father that she disapproved of his language. Vanya was not to be called a bum. The lecture that followed seemed to me—and perhaps to Father too—untimely, like correcting the grammar of someone who is trying to tell you the house is on fire. The lecture continued: Vanya was not to be called Vanya either. He must have a proper name. We were to introduce ourselves as usual, etc. Perhaps this man has a *worthy* reason for begging? Don't you *agree,* Samuel?

Father not only agreed, but having been rebuked, went on to remind me that we must not judge people by their appearance, etc., etc.

Fidgeting from foot to foot, I listened to everything they had to say, but as far as I was concerned, Vanya the bum was coming to live with us and I was not only terrified but revolted.

Perhaps the village housing chief would have a change of heart, I thought to myself.

The next evening, Vanya the bum stood at our open door.

"May I come in?"

"Of course you may." Mother stood up.

"Good evening." Father went toward Vanya.

"Good . . . evening." Vanya's response was tentative.

Regardless of all these amenities, this tall, bone-thin specter in filthy clothes, with dark bushy hair and a matted beard, was still a bum to me. But I felt Mother's eyes on me.

"Good evening," I said, going forward but keeping my hands rigidly at my sides. "My name is Esther Rudomin. What's yours?"

"Vanya."

His deeply sunken eyes darted from Mother to Father and back to me.

"My name is Ivan Petrovich, my child," he amended, and there was a tiny spark in his eyes.

"Welcome to our house, Ivan Petrovich," my father said.

For the first time, Grandmother, who had been watching this scene more or less huddled in her bed, spoke up. "Welcome," she murmured.

"Thank you, thank you. Where may I put down my stick? And this bag?" The bag was a tattered dusty bundle.

No one had given this matter a thought.

In a tiny room with a hole in its center and three of its corners already occupied by beds, the obvious answer was the fourth corner. But the intention had been to build the winter stove in that corner.

"So we will make the stove smaller," Mother said, answering our unspoken words, and pointed to the corner. "Maybe we can get some wood for a *nari,* like ours."

"Oh, please—don't worry about me. I'll be very comfortable just as it is." He smiled a little sardonically. "I beg your pardon for this intrusion. Your privacy—"

I could see that my parents and my grandmother

were as impressed as I was at his language and his accent: this was no illiterate.

Using his stick dexterously, he hobbled off to his corner on his one leg. There, he stretched out on the floor with his head on his bundle and said that he would rest.

It was an awkward moment. It was still early; what were we to do now? Just sit and watch this stranger rest?

"Please," he said with his eyes closed, "the child can sing and play and do anything she likes. When I am tired, I sleep and when I sleep, I sleep the sleep of the dead."

"Thank you," I said.

And I meant it. Living with a bum was going to be more agreeable than living with our former landladies, who were forever hushing me and the little boy.

The transformation from village bum to Ivan Petrovich did not take place overnight—either in my mind or in reality. At first he remained a shadowy figure from the dark world of the homeless, the friendless, the outcast. He left very early each morning and when he came home at night, he went directly to his corner—not that there was anyplace else to go. He talked very little, munched on bits of food he had picked up, and went to sleep. But before he ate, he always offered me anything he had brought—a fresh carrot, perhaps, or a beet. My parents always offered food in return, but he always refused. I, on the other hand, used to accept a bit of carrot or beet because I didn't want to hurt his feelings. Recently, Mother had amended her view of the etiquette for accepting precious food: When some was offered, you took a tiny bit if you thought they did not have enough, but that you took; it was only polite to do so.

After a few weeks had gone by, the transformation began: he started to eat with us, sharing whatever he had brought. If we cooked potatoes, we added his carrot to it and called it a vegetable stew. If it was a white beet, we boiled it until we could spread it on bread instead of jam.

Then he began to talk. Ivan Petrovich was a shoemaker from the Ukraine, a man who knew his craft and who had read many books. But once he had talked too much or too carelessly or had been misunderstood. He never did know why he had been sent to prison in Siberia; such a piece of information had been considered superfluous. And when he had been released, he had only one leg left and made his way from village to village begging.

Soon he began to wash himself, which pleased us more than it is polite to say. And to comb his beard. And to carry himself with dignity. He became Ivan Petrovich—for the time being at least.

When he first came to our house, we were the object of much curiosity: What is it like to have a bum in your house? Does he steal? How do you talk to a bum? How does he talk to you? Doesn't it make you shudder?

But as Ivan Petrovich came to regard himself differently, so did the villagers: he became much less a bum and much more just another human being cast off on the great Siberian steppe.

One day he disappeared. He left as usual early one morning and that was the last that any of us ever saw of Ivan Petrovich, formerly known as Vanya the bum.

The First Day of the War

by Maia Wojciechowska
(mī′ ä voi che hôv′skä)

*Some events make you grow up quickly.
They thrust you into new realms of
experience, forcing you to look at yourself
and others in new ways. As you read this
excerpt from Maia Wojciechowska's
autobiography, think about the discoveries
she makes in a time of crisis. How would
you compare Maia's feelings toward her
parents with Yoko's?*

It started like the best of all mornings. I woke up
from a dream to the sound of the plane.

He would often come early in the morning, and I
always knew he would not land before I got out of
bed and ran outside. While waiting, he would make
lazy circles in the sky. And as I rushed out, there
would always be an unasked question in my mind:
did he love fear more than freedom or freedom more
than fear? For he always did something frightening
that might end his freedom: rolls and spins and that
horrible, inevitable climb into the infinity of the sky.
Each time I saw him go vertically away from me, I
thought he wouldn't *want* to come down.

But he always did. And that descent, straight
down, the nose of the plane an arrow shooting the
earth, falling, gaining in loudness as he lost altitude,
made me catch my breath and forced my eyes to

close. Would he straighten up in time? Would a wing catch a treetop as it once did? But he was immortal. The plane might lose a wing or even burn, but nothing would happen to him. Not to my hero, my flying knight, my father.

Even as I raced against the landing plane, trying to reach it before he cut the engine, hoping that he would have time to take me up, trying not to be blown down by the great gusts of wind from the propeller blades, even as I climbed up to the cockpit, I was afraid. Afraid that he would be alone, unreachable, private in that world of his where I couldn't even be a trespasser. Even flying with him, beside him, even then he was still a fugitive from me.

Today was different. The sound of the plane was gone by the time I rushed outside. Then I heard another. Not just one but several planes were flying overhead. Next to me was my newest possession, one he had not yet seen—a Doberman puppy. The dog had no name yet. He was brand new, and I loved him. Yesterday, when I got him, he had run away from the vet who was going to trim his ears and cut his tail to a stump. The litter of five submitted yappingly to the operation, but not he. He tore himself away from me, and I chased him through a swamp, across what I was afraid was a bed of quicksand, wanting to catch him and yet also wanting him to get away. Now his black glistening body, for he had fallen into a puddle, was jumping over weeds and disappearing into the tall grass.

Now there was another plane. I looked up, but it wasn't his—it did not have white and red squared under the wings. The plane dipped down and flew low, parallel with my running dog. It slid down even lower, and there was a sound—a sound I didn't understand, a sound I had never heard before. As my dog leaped up, I saw him for a brief moment over the grass, shadowed by the plane's wing. Then the plane rose and flew away.

I stood in that field not moving, waiting for my dog to continue running in that sunlit place, which was at the edge of my summer world, but I couldn't see him anywhere. And there were no sounds—not one single sound since that sound that I was now beginning to understand. As I started to walk forward, I already knew what I would see, and knowing was evil and I wanted to take back what I knew.

I did not bury my dog. I did not touch him. I turned away from him because he did not move. He would never have a name.

I climbed a tree and sat there, trying not to think of anything, trying not to hate. But trying did no good, and I hated—everything I knew and everything that I didn't understand. I hated everyone, especially those who now were making noises inside my house. I hated the car that had pulled in front of the house and its running, sputtering engine. And most of all I hated my mother's voice calling my name and the slamming of the doors. And I hated the summer for having so suddenly ended.

When I got tired of hating, I came down off the tree and swore to myself that nobody would ever know what had happened to my dog. I promised not to say anything to anyone, not until I understood why and who had done it. Not until I found a way of paying them back. Not until after I killed the one who had killed him.

A man I never liked, a friend of my mother's, was yelling at me that I was lucky I wasn't being left behind. I stuck my tongue out at him when he turned his back and told my mother there was no time to pack anything. He pulled her and pushed me toward the car, where my brothers were already seated, both of them sleepy and angry. I didn't dare protest against this kidnapping of my person because I was afraid that if I opened my mouth, I'd cry.

I remembered from way back that every time I felt hurt, I had to do something mean, as if being mean could in itself cure the hurt. I took away a roll my little brother Krzys (kris) was eating and threw it out of the car window. And when he, aged six, began to cry, I placed my hand over his mouth. He knew better than to struggle against me. But I could feel his tears on my hand, for he was crying over his loss while I couldn't cry over mine. I consoled myself with the thought that I have a devil inside me and that I would go straight to hell when I die.

The car was taking me away from the field where my dog was lying dead and would be eaten by buzzards before noon. There was a loud argument in the car about the war. Zbyszek (zbi'shǝk), my fourteen-year-old brother, was insisting that we were certainly going to win and especially because he planned to enlist in the Polish Air Force. The man at the wheel was of the opinion that Poland had no chance to defend itself against Germany. And my mother, pulling on a pair of white gloves, expressed her disbelief that the war should have started at such an inconvenient time. We were going to go back to France next week. And I began to laugh. I laughed loud and hard because at twelve I was glad my country was at war with people who shot down dogs.

I realized it would be hard to find him, the one who actually did kill my dog. Maybe I could advertise. "Wanted: The German pilot who shot down a Doberman pup on September 1, 1939.

Important reward." He'd answer the ad and I'd be ready for him. I had stolen a book from a Paris bookstore about medieval tortures. It was behind in the house, but I remembered most of them. He would be a long time dying. Water dripping first, then bamboo spikes, or better still nails, rusty and long, under the fingernails. Hot coals and scalding water. I could pull out his hair by the handfuls, or maybe I could even build a rack or a pendulum. What would be nicest of all would be to have him die behind a horse and be dragged around for miles, face down, across fields stubby with weeds, coarse with stones. Or maybe I could find a mad dog and let him be bitten to death. That would be poetic justice.

We were in a sixth-floor apartment in Warsaw. The view from here was fantastic. It was too good to be true. People down below on the street were running in circles; cars, buses, and trolleys were piling up, being abandoned; furniture and suitcases were all over the sidewalks. And in the distance there were several fires. The sirens went on again—I was getting used to their shrieks—and all activities stopped as the sound of the planes came into the apartment through the windows I flung open.

"Why did he leave us here?" My mother kept repeating the question, although my brother had told her several times that the reason her friend locked us in this place was that he wanted to steal from us. Especially the new car, the one my father had just brought into Poland from France—a splendid, new, custom-made Delage. I hated to listen to them, so I leaned farther out of the window and was glad when the bombs began to fall. I grabbed Krzys by the hand and dragged him to the window, and we began to imitate the sounds of the bomb. First the plane's engine, then the whistle of the falling bomb, and then its great triumphant explosion. "BOOM!" We laughed like crazy, and Mother suddenly realized we were in "mortal danger" and ordered us to hide under the sofa. I accused her of "sudden senility," which had recently become my favorite expression of disdain, and explained as haughtily as possible that if we were going to be hit, I'd feel much safer falling down six floors than having a sofa come on my head.

"We should be in a shelter," she answered with little logic since she'd tried the door several times and found it locked. Her friend assured us we'd be safe here. She always had a hard time coming to grips with reality and a harder time distrusting people or seeing herself being taken advantage of.

But I couldn't be bothered with her now. The view out of the window was fascinating. Houses collapsed, churches crumbled. Someone, maybe God Himself, had started the biggest game in the world, and I couldn't wait to get involved.

While Zbyszek attacked the door, trying to break it down, I invented a game for Krzys. We broke everything we could get our hands on, and what we couldn't break, we threw out of the window. My mother was carrying on a semi-hysterical monologue and didn't even notice when the house across the street, almost as tall as the one we were in, was hit directly, collapsed in slow motion and in a great cloud of dust as we were flung down by the explosion. There was broken glass all over the floor now, and the bookcase had fallen not two feet away from my mother. Krzys began to cry, and I hit him because I didn't want to give the Germans the satisfaction of making any of us cry. For suddenly I knew something else—I knew about wars. It started with the killing of dogs, but then it all became a matter of pride, of winning over fear.

The door opened, and the man who had locked us in was back telling us that he had seen my father. I tried to hear every word he said about him, but Zbyszek was yelling at him accusations of thievery, and my mother was asking silly questions about danger from bombs. I pieced together the information about my father; he had been ordered to go to London and Paris to ask for reinforcements for the Polish Air Force. He had taken a plane and was piloting it himself. We were to get a train, go through Rumania to France, where we were to join him because he was ordered not to come back to Poland.

My father had done it again—abandoned us, freed himself from us! Not even a war could stop him from flying away. I hit my fist against the doorframe and wished everyone dead so that I could cry in peace over this news, over life's inhumanity to me.

How many times have I cried over my father without anyone's knowing about it? Each birthday and each name day because he was never there. And whenever it rained. I cried for him inside the dark movie houses when I watched sad films and over books that were not even sad. Only once—how old was I, nine or eight?—I cried in front of him. I had torn up a dress my mother had made for me. A horrid taffeta dress, loud with noises, full of ribbons and bows and laced petticoats. I had hated being a girl and wished to have nothing to do with dresses like that. I tore it off, tore it apart, threw it at her, and went to hide my anger over her attempts to brand me a girl. He had found me in the garden on a swing. He had his belt in his hands, and he hit me with it half a dozen times. Not hard, but he hit me. For the first and only time. And I had cried. Then he talked to me, for the first time, about being cruel to my mother and thoughtless. And I cried. Not because he had hit me. Not because of what he said. Not because of what I was, and I was cruel and thoughtless. I cried because he did not know this firsthand but had learned it just then—from his wife.

He didn't know anything about me. He didn't know that I had always wanted to be a boy because being a boy would have made me closer to being like him when I grew up. He did not know about the time Zbyszek's friends had tied me to a tombstone and left me overnight in the cemetery. He didn't know that once the same boys tied me up to a tree, built a pile of sticks under my feet, and dared me to scream as they lit it. He did not know that I told them that not only would I not scream, but also that I would, if they untied my hands, light the fire myself so that they would not get into trouble. He did not know that I had been scared the time he finally allowed me to jump from an airplane, and that I had been lying to him that day, for I had changed my mind and didn't want to jump. He did not know that for a moment, before the chute opened, I wished that God would not let me die before I told my father that I loved him more than life. He didn't know my hates or my longings or my loves, or the fact that I could not fall asleep without reading to myself under the covers. He didn't know that I was jealous of everyone he had time for. He didn't know that I always wanted him to be proud of me. He didn't know my dog had been killed that morning. He didn't know he shouldn't have left us.

Generations

by Amy Lowell

Amid the chaos of wartorn Korea, Yoko's relationship with her mother grows stronger and stronger. As you read this poem, think about the relationship between the speaker and the person addressed. How would you compare this relationship with the one between Yoko and her mother?

You are like the stem
Of a young beech-tree,
Straight and swaying,
Breaking out in golden leaves.
5   Your walk is like the blowing of a beech-tree
On a hill.
Your voice is like leaves
Softly struck upon by a South wind.
Your shadow is no shadow, but a scattered
   sunshine;
10 And at night you pull the sky down to you
And hood yourself in stars.

But I am like a great oak under a cloudy sky,
Watching a stripling beech grow up at my
   feet.

The Key

by Võ Phiên
*translated from the Vietnamese
by Phan Phan*

*Like Yoko and her family—and refugees
anywhere—the narrator of this story has
left loved ones behind. Written by a
refugee from Vietnam, this story is really a
story within a story. As you read, think
about what the story suggests about the
plight of refugees.*

To say that the first picture in the memories of the
wanderings of an unfortunate man who has lost his
country and left everything behind is a shower seems
ridiculous. What a strange recollection. Perhaps I
should say something sorrowful, more poetic. But
how can I? None could take refuge the way he
wished.

We came to U.S. territory at night. Despite our
excited state, darkness prohibited a clear view of part
of a country we were going to spend the rest of our
life in. At that late hour the island of Guam seemed
to consist of thousands of lights.

Our ship dropped anchor about 3 a.m., July 5,
1975. We, nine thousand people, gathered on deck,
confused at first. Then, one by one, we climbed
down the rope ladder. One man led his son by the
hand, another carried his old father; one carried his
briefcase, another wrapped his property in a blanket
and another loosely held a water container in his
hand. One was really naked, wearing only underwear.

These poor people were warmly received. Not only were U.S. military officers waiting at the port, there were also Red Cross workers, local authorities and some church leaders.

I watched the beginning of the exodus into the foreign land from the deck of the American Challenger. The refugees proceeded slowly into the well-dressed crowd. Everyone, whether Christian or not, was deeply moved by the presence of an old bishop on the deck in the early morning hours.

My fellow countrymen passed by the important persons cautiously. Carrying sleeping mats and blankets, fathers and sons walked together quietly for nearly fifty feet and then they caught sight of the signs to . . . the showers! Yes, there were the Showers.

The first showers we saw in America stood there in open air. So from the deck I watched people, old and young, quickly undress, rub off the dirt and splash under the showers. Taking a bath so hurriedly at that hour, close to such a solemn setting! I felt lost. "Yes, even in this country, sanitary measures went along with the warmest feelings. Good."

In my country, there is an expression, "rubbing off the dirt." In honor of a friend or relative who just returned from a trip, we might have a party or a dinner "to rub the dirt off from the long journey." The word "dirt" is, of course, used figuratively. And so, I compared the rubbing-off-the-dirt feast in my country with the way people rub off the dirt with soap and water here and could not help but worry for the vast differences between the two cultures.

During our stay in tents on Orote Points, the baths at those open air showers became an important part of our daily activities. From early morning until late afternoon, in the hot sun, people lined up to get to the showers. The gatherings around the showers were quite interesting. With 5, 6 or 7 persons in a small wooden room—four rooms standing next to each other—we could look at the sky above, watch the slowly drifting clouds and make conversation with new friends. We discussed many things: the ceremony of lowering the Vietnamese flag on a warship before entering the Subic Bay; the flavor of the ham we'd just eaten; the last days of the nation; getting milk for the babies, etc. Valuable experiences were exchanged, unexpected stories of the fates of friends and relatives were shared under the showers at Orote Points.

In contrast, we had another kind of bathroom at the Fort Indiantown Gap, Pennsylvania, refugee camp. There, each section had about 100 people with only a small shower, a pitch dark, stifling shower with no window. There was no door either; just a curtain. In that small room, there were three showers so that three people of the same sex could take baths at the same time. There was a cardboard hanging on a curtain with one side reading "Men" and the other "Women." To avoid serious mistakes, one has to check and put out the appropriate side before using the shower.

As the shower was airtight, some people used it as a fumigator. If one caught a cold, he came into the room, then turned on the shower and stepped aside to avoid the hot water. The steam would rise, the man would be soaked with perspiration and eventually would feel much better.

The shower was also used for recording. The refugees were thirsty for musical tapes. Each family tried to get some familiar songs and favorite voices before they left the camp. Some thought of the shower. About midnight, when most of us had fallen asleep, when all the noises had quieted, one could bring two cassette recorders into the showers. Yes, this was the place for tape recording. With a few borrowed tapes, two recorders together, one as a transmitter, the other as a receiver, the country music lover could continue his work until the next morning.

And it was in the bathroom that I had the chance to listen to the confessions of a man in his mid-fifties.

He was an extremely shy, cautious man. Ordinarily, he seldom talked to anyone in an open manner. Nearly all of us had suffered many heartbreaking losses. Everyday, we moaned, talked on and on while the ladies often cried. Being together for a while, we came to understand the circumstances of others pretty soon, at least in a general way: This lady, wife of a colonel, could get out but her husband and sons got stuck in Vietnam; that fellow, student of the School of Agriculture, ran for his life from B. to N. province, then from N. to Saigon and met a rescue ship there and now his parents won't know what happened to him; or the family of that wealthy businessman hurriedly climbed on an American ship, leaving behind gold and dollars which could be worth millions of piasters; and so on . . .

However, I didn't know exactly what had happened to the family of that old man.

His was a complete family of husband and wife, a daughter and two sons. It was good enough, for who could expect to have brothers and sisters, aunts and uncles to go with? Yet, there was grief and apprehension on the couple's faces. That concern overruled their surroundings and even spoiled the liveliness of their young sons.

I'd wanted to ask him many times. But at the same

time I found that it was not an easy thing to do. I wondered if it might be too curious or crude, especially to a man like him. Besides, he didn't need us; he seemed to be trying to avoid our friendliness.

In fact, I had hardly ever met such a shy man. He was as shy as a girl who just reached maturity. He spoke good English, and it was rumored that he'd been an English teacher for many years. At the refugee camp's main office, he was sometimes asked to do translation for other people. On such occasions he was even more bashful. If someone said something, he listened and remained quiet for a while. He would look at us questioningly as though it was too bold to say. And perhaps, for him, everything was too bold. He'd hesitate again until someone reminded, "Please translate it for me." And again, his attitude was the same.

Would it be too daring to ask anything from such a man?

And then, one night about 11 o'clock, I went to the shower. As I stood in front of the curtain, I read the sign: "Men" and could hear the sound of splashing water inside. I asked, "Who's in there? May I come in?"

A cheerful voice replied, "Sure. Please come in."

Raising the curtain, I recognized the shy man immediately. He was unusually kind to me.

"Hello! Feel free, please. More people, more fun. Ha, ha."

He was "feeling free" in the shower, indeed. He was naked and covered with soapsuds. Vietnamese laws do not require a person to cover a particular part of his body in front of someone else, but we don't, however, get accustomed to being nude at public baths as the Japanese do. His attitude really encouraged me. I then started "feeling free."

While I was taking off my clothes, my new friend continued to talk, asking question after question: "When did you leave Saigon? Oh, really? April 29? Half a day earlier than us, then. Which street did you live on? H. Street? We had an uncle who lived on that very street. We used to visit him quite frequently . . . Might have passed by your house, who knows? Ha, Ha. When did you come here? Applied for a sponsor yet? Which one? . . ."

I was amazed and delighted. It seemed to me this man was completely different from the one I had known before. From one topic to another, my friend talked and talked in a cheerful mood while rubbing his body. We treated each other like long time old friends. I soon realized that sometimes displaying human bodies eventually led to displaying human hearts. Once getting rid of all the clumsy clothes, of all artificial relationships, suddenly feeling free, man in the shower would no longer be afraid of any daring act.

Finally, he talked about his own trip:

"My father is 93 years old now. My wife and I had thought about it over and over since N. province was lost. Surely it was time to run away, but what about my father? He's too old and weak to bear any hazard we might encounter during evacuation. As for us, we ran for our lives, not for any trip, didn't we? On the other hand, we wouldn't have peace of mind leaving him alone! I have a younger sister who lived in D. province. Since the loss of that province, I haven't heard anything from her; she's dead or alive, or where is she living now? I don't know. Oh yes, I still have a few cousins, a few nephews and nieces, but they all planned to go. It's hard to find someone to take care of him. To tell you the truth, it's been six years that my father has become more and more senile. He's absent minded and sometimes behaves like a child. Poor father. Whenever he thought about his own age, he asked me to buy a coffin for him."

"A coffin?"

"Yes. A coffin. Traditionally, old men asked for a coffin ready at any time. But that usually happened more in rural areas. Who dares to put a coffin in his home if he lives in the city? It would look terrible, especially since our children cannot accept old customs and habits. That's why we had to keep promising him a coffin, a real good one for when he passed away. Yet people said that if anyone died during the evacuation, the body would be thrown into the sea. As you can see, how could we urge him to throw himself in danger?

"Finally, our relatives met to solve the problem. We concluded that it was almost certain that not all of us would be able to get out. Therefore, anyone who stayed would take care of my father. On the other hand, if we could all get out, the friends and neighbors would be asked for help. All the money and valuable things would belong to those who stayed with my father.

"And then, on April 29, with him seated in a big chair in the living room, all of us, one by one, bowed and thanked him, saying goodbye. We knew this would be goodbye forever.

"What the military situation is, what is happening in the country, what his descendants are trying to do, and so on, I'm sure my father is not clear-sighted enough to understand. But, strangely enough, he could feel that something extraordinary, something tragic, was going on. Yes sir, he sat in the chair with tears flowing gently down his cheeks. We tried to comfort him, but he didn't say anything.

"Later, we packed our luggage. We hid all the

money and valuables in a wardrobe and locked it up. An ounce of gold was set aside for buying his coffin. Anybody, friend or neighbor, who decides to take care of him, was entitled to all we left. We couldn't put it all in his pockets as it would be too hazardous for him.

"When we had prepared everything, around 8 p.m., he was still sleeping. It was painful to watch him sleep in the bed, his body all curled up like a small child. We hesitated for a while and then walked away. Waking him up at that time would be a heart-breaking thing to do.

"At that time, enemy forces had advanced into some areas of the city, and the situation was critical. We didn't even know if we could make it out.

"A friend of ours organized the evacuation program which would take place at the port of H. The small boat was so overcrowded that many times, I thought we would not survive. After three days of struggling for survival, on May 2 we were rescued by an American ship in the international territorial waters. We knew then we'd escaped death.

"But sir, it was right at that moment that I was shocked. As I was checking my luggage, I put my hand into my pocket and found that in my hurry I had forgotten to leave the key to the wardrobe for him. My God, I put all the money along with gold and jewelry in the wardrobe, then locked it up!

"I remained silent awhile. Then, gradually, various things appeared in my mind: my father's confusion when he woke up, finding himself alone in the empty house; the scene of our relatives and friends coming in, asking for money we had left; questions about the 'hidden key' would be raised; the scene of smashing the wardrobe would frighten him. And thieves and robbers might come in and assault or beat him up.

What made me so stupid, so absent minded like that
. . . hic!"

The man stopped. He was choking on water
maybe. I could hear just the sound of running water.
Then he continued:

"My friend, since then I have been obsessed by
those terrible pictures. From day to day, month to
month, I never feel relieved. God has punished us,
you see. I'm so stupid. Hic. I brought the key with
me. Hic."

The man stopped again. The water stopped
running simultaneously. He had finished his shower.
His hands were searching for the towel. Having
accustomed my eyes to the dark, I could see his
shoulders tremble gently. The man wiped the water
from his body and the tears from his eyes.

When did he cry? When I thought he had choked
on water? But he was dressing hurriedly as though he
was trying to run away. As he stretched his hands out
to put his shirt on, I saw a key hanging on a string.
There, my old friend carried his key where a
Christian typically wears a picture of his God.

Remaining alone in the bathroom, I stood
motionless for a while. Then I turned off the water,
dressed, raised the curtain and left. Most people had
gone back to their rooms and were asleep.

It was a quiet night. The moon was bright in a
clear sky. I looked at the shiny moon, touching
lightly the key in my hand. Yes, I had a key, kept in
my pocket, from a situation similar to that of the old
man. (In fact, isn't it true that most of the refugees
brought a key along? I mean, who did not feel sorry
for a certain mistake, a certain shortcoming he had
made to his relatives and close friends who were left

behind, something he would feel sorry for the rest of his wandering life?)

Later, a few times, I tried to tell my own story to that man, but it was not easy as he had returned to the attitude he had had before, extremely quiet and shy. Sometimes, I thought he avoided me as though he was avoiding the same mistake or seeing a bad moment in his life again.

I didn't have a chance to meet him again in the shower.

Please Don't Leave

A Hmong love song

by Mr. Lue Lee

*As Yoko discovers, war exacts a terrible
toll, filling families with dread that they
may never again see the faces they love.
In this poem, a Hmong love song, the
speaker describes what it is like to say
goodbye.*

Even though I smile on the outside,
Inside my heart I cry, please don't leave.
I want us to stay together forever,
Like the sun and the moon.
5 My heart is rushing and broken,
Like a wild river,
My heart, my feelings, are like the moving
    clouds,
Always changing, with no place to rest.
My Beloved, is there any day, or any way,
10 That we will meet again?
Will our separation be for days?
Or will it be for months?
Please, let us meet again before we die.
Wherever you go,
15 I hope you have a happy life,
Free of sorrow.
No matter what happens,
I will miss you forever.